CLASSIC COUNTRY MUSIC

TRIVIA QUIZ

CLASSIC COUNTRY MUSIC

TRIVIA QUIZ

by
MARK KNICKELBINE

BowerHouseBooks.com

Cover Design by Margaret McCullough
Text Design by Rebecca Finkel
Printed in Canada

Library of Congress Control Number: 2008927580

Paperback ISBN: 978-1-934553-07-7

10 9 8 7 6 5 4 3 2

TABLE OF
Contents

Fiddle players were the first successful country recording artists,
and Fiddlin' John Carson was radio's first "hillbilly" star.

CHAPTER ONE

Country Roots

Fans of classic country often insist on their preference for "real hillbilly music." But where did country really come from? We like to imagine Ma and Pa sitting on the porch of their cabin in the hills, strumming a banjo and guitar and singing some ancient folk song dating back to Celtic Britain. And it's true that the roots of country run through the homemade songs and dance tunes passed from one generation of rural southerners to another.

But reality is a little more complicated than the rustic myth. For one thing, not many rural white people played banjos and guitars until the early 20th century, after they were popularized by the descendents of African slaves. And the song Ma and Pa were singing was just as likely to be a modern invention written by Tin Pan Alley songwriters in New York. While the instruments and songs of old Europe lived on in the Appalachian hills, from the very start country music was a blend of old and new, folk and commercial, black and white.

Rather than search for a mythical "real" country music, it's more interesting to listen to country as part of the great American musical melting pot, in which a unique set of musical influences in a particular place and time came together to create a new form that is loved today around the world. Right from the start, country music was an expression of a yearning for the truths and feelings of the golden past, a past that was never more vivid than it was in the songs themselves.

True or false? The country classic, "The Wildwood Flower," with its strange Elizabethan lyrics, was originally a folk song brought to America from either England or Ireland.

 False. Like other such songs—"The Rosewood Casket," "Letter Edged in Black," and so on—"Wildwood Flower" was written by American songwriters, primarily to appeal to urban audiences in the North. Maud Irving and Joseph Philbrick Webster wrote this "folk song" in 1860.

 You're in Amarillo in 1868 listening to a showman sing "The Yellow Rose of Texas." What kind of makeup is he likely to be wearing?

 Blackface, usually something like charcoal or black greasepaint designed to make white people look like "darkies." It was the standard makeup of the minstrel show, a kind of itinerant act based on very stylized stereotypes of black people. Combining rustic humor and music, minstrel shows were wildly popular throughout America well into the 20th century, and were one of the main ways that popular music traveled to the hollers and cotton towns of the South.

What was a "physic wagon"?

We remember them as medicine shows, another form of traveling entertainment that brought songs to people who didn't live anywhere near an opera house or vaudeville theatre. The medicine show wagon would roll into the main square of a little town, and a band would strike up a tune; soon a crowd would gather around to enjoy the singers, comedians, magic acts, freaks, and any of a wild and weird variety of acts such shows might offer. Then, of course, came the sales pitch for whatever kind of wonder cure was being pushed (often a concoction of pine tar and grain alcohol).

Thanks to minstrel and medicine shows, southern country folk were exposed to much of the same popular music available to people in the North. What kind of music, which later became a cornerstone of country, could southerners hear in the late 19th century that northerners couldn't?

The blues, and the African American spirituals and work songs that were its predecessors. Although whites disdained blacks as people, they loved black music. One of the reasons for the development of the minstrel show was that it gave white people a chance to perform and listen to the music of African Americans without actually having to socialize with them.

In 1947, a blackface duo by the name of Jamup and Honey were part of a traveling tent show touring the South. What was it called?

 The "Grand Ole Opry" It was one of the traveling shows sent out from the Mother Church to take advantage of the popularity of the radio program. The most famous blackface act was Freeman Gosden and Charles Correll, whose *Amos 'n' Andy* characters were the stars of radio's earliest and most popular comedy series.

 There was a thriving music industry in the South well before records were available commercially. What did it sell?

 Sheet music. Without any mass media other than print, rural people had to make their own music, whether at home or at church. Everybody sang, and most homes had some kind of instrument—a piano, if you were lucky, or perhaps a fiddle or mandolin. All this homegrown musical activity created a demand for new songs to sing and play, and printed songbooks sold by the thousands. They were often peddled by traveling salesmen who would set up in a public place and perform the tunes as an inducement to get people to buy the songbooks.

What was a "Sankey"?

 That's the term that gradually adhered to the songs featured in one of the most popular songbooks of the late 19th century, Ira Sankey and P.P. Bliss's *Gospel Hymns*. It contained hymns that were heard at the camp revival meetings of the day. Sankey's compositions earned him the nickname "The Sweet Singer of Methodism."

 What religious movement that grew out of the Methodist revivals became a major disseminator of music throughout the rural South?

 The Holiness movement, also known as Pentecostalism. Pentecostal preachers spread throughout the South with highly emotional sermons calling for conversion and repentance. A big part of that appeal was the music, hymns that used folk, popular and even black music elements to generate a tremendous emotional response from their audience. Along with the shouting and swooning characteristic of Pentecostal meetings, this combination of "profane" music with sacred themes scandalized polite society—a conflict that would remain part of the heritage of country music.

Besides circulating the revival songs, what did *Gospel Hymns* contribute to American music?

The kind of popular, sentimental compositions it contained came to be known as gospel music, thanks to the booklet's title. Southern gospel music developed alongside country music and the two genres maintain a close relationship today.

The poor, unschooled folks who wanted to sing gospel songs typically couldn't read music. What replaced notes in the sheet music printed for such singers?

Shapes. In "shape-note" music notation, each note in the scale has a distinctive shape that the singer learns to associate with a particular sung tone. Thanks to shape-note music, a group of musically illiterate people can quickly learn to sing a song together in multiple-part harmony. An entire industry grew up around shape-note music, with singers and vocal groups giving singing lessons to teach the notation and sell their songbooks.

What famous country standard, the lyrics of which begin with watching Mama being carried away in a hearse, began as a shape-note hymn?

"Will the Circle be Unbroken" started off as Ada R. Habershon and Charles Gabriel's shape-note hymn "Can the Circle be Unbroken (Bye and Bye)."

True or False? The fiddle-playing styles in the South and Appalachia were part of an ancient tradition stretching back to the Celtic music of the British Isles.

 True enough. One of the genuinely European folk foundations of country music is the fiddle, which played dance music for the masses since its forebears found their way from China and the Middle East to Europe in the 10th century. The modern violin was invented in the late 16th century, just in time for the colonization of America. The portable instrument was easy for European immigrants to bring to the New World, and the jigs, reels, and ballads it played came along too.

 How did the countrified violin come to be called a "fiddle"?

 As with so much else in the development of the English language, it's a case of different words used by different social classes. The original root for both violin and fiddle is the Latin word *vitula*, meaning "stringed instrument." For cultured Latin speakers, the word evolved into the Italian "violin"; for rustic speakers of Germanic languages, it became the English "fiddle."

Name the instrument with West African roots that became a country music staple.

 The banjo. Slaves created homemade instruments from large gourds; Thomas Jefferson noted the "banjar" played by his plantation slaves in 1781. The manufactured, drum-headed, round-bodied banjo appeared with the minstrel shows; they were fretless and had only four strings.

 A Virginia minstrel by the name of Joel Walker Sweeney created a major banjo innovation in 1860. What was it?

 The addition of the 5th string. Placing a high-pitched string at the "top" of the neck allows the player to use his or her thumb to pluck a high note in a repeated pattern, creating a drone effect that gives banjo pickin' its distinctive sound.

 Name the innovation in the 1880s that further enhanced the banjo's appeal to the masses.

Frets. As any string player can tell you, the hardest part of learning to play a fretless instrument like the violin or the original banjo is figuring out how to find the notes. When frets were added to the banjo, anyone could quickly learn a few simple chords and start playing.

Another foundational country instrument had been brought to America by Europeans, but was popularized among rural southern audiences by black musicians. Name it.

 The guitar. Guitars were popular parlor instruments among the gentry, but the formalized style of playing and high-culture air associated with the instrument didn't interest country folk. Black musicians discovered the versatility of the cheap, portable guitar, which was quite similar to the lute-like instruments of African origin. They worked it into the blues early in the 20th century, and that's where many southerners first heard the guitar.

 Many purists think you ain't listening to country unless you're hearing an instrument introduced to American audiences by Hawaiians in the early 20th century. What is it?

 The steel guitar. The Hawaiians got guitars from the whites who came to the islands to raise cattle, and discovered that metal bars could be used to fret the strings. One story of its invention has a boy walking along the railroad tracks with his guitar, picking up a rail spike and applying it to the strings. By the 1920s, Hawaiian music, often with swinging jazz influences, was a huge fad in the United States. Hawaiian acts were often part of the traveling shows that brought music to country folk in the South.

What's steel about a steel guitar?

 It's not the strings or the body; it's the bar, usually made of stainless steel, that is used to fret the strings. The bar allows the steel guitar player to create all kinds of neat musical effects, from broad vibratos to sweeping glissandos to expressive bending of notes.

 Who were the first fans of commercialized Southern folk music?

 Northerners. Long before the Civil War, Americans in the Northern states were fascinated by the idea of the Sunny South. "Dixie" was celebrated in popular song as a mythical land where the old folks were at home way down upon the Sewanee (it's no accident that both "Dixie" and "Old Folks at Home" were written by northerners). In the early 20th century, northern musicologists like Cecil Sharp and Alan Lomax went out to the hills and hollers looking for real southern folk music and published it largely for an audience north of the Mason-Dixon line. Sharp's *Folksongs from the Southern Appalachians,* published in 1917, was the first real country music you could buy.

Who made the first country record, and when?

A fiddler from Hamlin, Texas, by the name of Eck Robertson, and his piano-playing partner, Henry Gilliland, showed up at the offices of the Victor Talking Machine Company in 1922 and convinced them to let them make some records. The records were hits, and country fiddle music became a hot commodity for record companies in the 1920s. Robertson made only a few more recordings and then disappeared from the national scene. He lived to see the rise of the country music industry and saw his own star rise again as part of the folk music revival of the 1960s.

Besides his historic recordings, Robertson broke ground on another enduring country music tradition. What was it?

Despite the fact that he worked as a piano tuner, Robertson put on cowboy garb to perform, including a broad-brimmed topper, thus becoming country music's first "hat act."

The next year, 1923, another fiddler, this one from Georgia, recorded "The Little Old Log Cabin in the Lane" for Okeh Records; it sold 500 copies in a month. Who was this musician, and why were his records so popular?

 It was John William Carson, known to his many fans as "Fiddlin' John." A seven-time winner of the Georgia Old Time Fiddlers Association contest, Fiddlin' John had already built quite a following playing dances and political rallies by the time he became a regular performer on Atlanta radio station WSB in 1922. Carson was therefore one of the very first country acts ever broadcast, and that exposure made him the first commercially successful country recording act as well.

 While we're talking about the wireless, what distinction did WSB hold? And what do its call letters stand for?

 With its inaugural broadcast on March 15, 1922, WSB became the first commercial radio station in the South. The call letters stand for "Welcome South, brother." By the mid-1920s, radios became cheap enough for working class families to afford, and the birth of country as a popular music genre paralleled the rise of the new medium.

The National Life and Accident Insurance Company, whose slogan was "We Shield Millions," started a radio station in its headquarters town of Nashville, Tennessee, in 1925. What were its call letters, and why should country fans care?

 National Life took its call letters from the initials of its slogan. WSM soon hired George D. Hay, who began programming old-time music acts, including a regular Saturday night program Hay would come to call *The Grand Ole Opry*. More about that later.

 A string band from the hills of Virginia and North Carolina made their first recordings in 1925 and later became the first country act to perform in New York City. They are largely forgotten today, but they made a lasting contribution to the evolution of country music. Who were they?

 Al and John Hopkins, Charlie Bowman, and Tony Alderman made six recordings for Okeh Records in New York, and the company needed a name to put on the record labels. "Call the band anything you want," Al Hopkins told them. "We're nothing but a bunch of hillbillies anyway." The band became the Hill Billies, the first time the term was associated with the music genre. Soon, "hillbilly music" became the standard label for the commercialized southern folk sound, long before anyone began referring to it as "country."

What other firsts could the Hill Billies claim?

They were the first country act to use a Hawaiian steel guitar, and the first to appear in a motion picture.

Pop singer Vernon Dalhart began making modestly successful records in 1916, but by 1924 his popularity was waning, and he needed something to juice up his career. What did he do?

He turned to country music, and with the hits "The Wreck of the Old 97" and "The Prisoner's Song," became a huge star. The record containing the two songs, released by the Edison Company, sold more than a million copies. From 1925 to 1931, Dalhart made hundreds of records, including many re-recordings of his first two hillbilly hits, and was one of the most commercially successful acts of early country music.

Name the song:
Oh, I wish I had someone to love me
Someone to call me their own
Oh, I wish I had someone to live with
'Cause I'm tired of livin' alone.

"The Prisoner's Song," written by Guy Massey in 1924. Its verses, drawn from a variety of prison work songs, also contain the famous lines, *If I had the wings of an angel/Over these prison walls I would fly.*

The popularity of the first hillbilly recordings was one reason why companies like Edison, Victor, Brunswick, and Okeh issued so many of them. What was the other principal reason?

They were cheap to make. The pop, classical, opera, and brass band numbers that were standard recording fare required many musicians and lots of studio time to record, all of which cost money. As record sales declined with the rise of radio, the record companies needed ways to enhance their profits. With hillbilly music, two or three musicians with a few string instruments could record numbers quickly and cheaply, thus increasing the record company's bottom line.

Name the banjoist and comedian who became the first star of the *Grand Ole Opry*, which he joined in 1926.

Uncle Dave Macon, who often danced along to his own accompaniment, hooting and hollering as he did. Already in his fifties when he began his recording and radio career, Uncle Dave went on entertaining audiences with his energetic, down-home style right up until his death in 1952.

What was Uncle Dave's first regular gig?

He was a vaudeville entertainer. A mule drover by profession, he had played neighbors' parties and local dances for years. In 1918, a talent scout for the Lowe's Theatre circuit spotted him, and his career as an entertainer began.

What was the original name of the *Grand Ole Opry?* And how did it get its famous appellation?

By 1927, Nashville's WSM featured a regular, three-hour program of hillbilly acts on Saturday nights, called the *WSM Barn Dance,* which immediately followed the pedantic classical program, *Musical Appreciation Hour.* One evening, noting the rather jarring transition between high classics and hillbilly twang, George D. Hay announced, "For the past hour, we have been listening to music taken largely from grand opera, but from now on we will present the grand ole opry."

By creating the *Opry,* Hay was a major figure in spreading the music of hillbilly string bands to the world and was a founder of the country music industry. Where was he born?

Hay was a midwestern native; he was born in Attica, Indiana, in 1895. He didn't live in the South until he moved to Memphis after being discharged from the army.

What was George D. Hay's nickname, and how did he acquire it?

 Hay started off as a reporter for the *Commercial Appeal,* a Memphis newspaper. He covered the courthouse beat, and created a popular column, "Howdy, Judge," which relayed humorous conversations between country bumpkins and the judge. Although he was only in his 20s, he picked up the nickname, "The Solemn Ole Judge." When his newspaper started a radio station in 1923, Hay became one of its announcers, and his radio career was launched.

 George D. Hay had another gig with what would become the very first nationally broadcast country radio program. What was it called?

 It began in 1924 as the *WLS Barn Dance*; originating from the powerful Chicago radio station, it could be heard throughout much of the Midwest. Its reach was enhanced even further in 1933, when NBC began carrying an hour of the program nationwide, and the show was renamed the *National Barn Dance.* Early country stars like Patsy Montana and Lulu Belle & Scotty were thus introduced to a national audience. On radio and television, the program survived in one form or another until 1971.

One of Hay's many gimmicks was a steamboat whistle that he blew to start off the show. What was the steamboat whistle's name?

 Hushpuckena.

 Beginning in 1927, five-string banjo player Dock Boggs began recording tunes with a distinct African-American sound. Where had Boggs learned black music?

 Working alongside blacks in the coal mines of the Virginia hills. A coal miner since the age of 12, Boggs took to the banjo and was signed by the Brunswick Records label when they came to the area to audition "mountain talent" in 1927.

 Besides his material, what other influence did Boggs pick up from black musicians?

 His banjo playing style, quite distinct from the thumb and finger strumming technique used by most hillbilly banjo players, known as "frailing." Instead, Boggs used a finger-picking style that allowed him to play melodic lines full of soulful bent notes reminiscent of blues guitar players.

What's the next line?
Come dig a hole in the meadow good people
Come dig a hole in the ground
Then come around, all you good people . . .

 . . . and see this poor rambler go down.
These lyrics from Dock Boggs's "Country Blues" are similar
to a verse in many versions of the song "Darlin' Corey."

Maybelle, A.P., and Sara Carter, the original Carter Family.

CHAPTER TWO

The Carters and Jimmie Rodgers

By the late 1920s, country music was becoming a commercial force, and its first two star acts were Jimmie Rodgers and the Carter Family. Neither sounds much like the country string bands that came before them, or the honky-tonk stars of country's heyday. Yet all the elements we associate with classic country were there: the mix of sacred and profane love in the Carter Family's songs; the modal harmonies that blended their voices; Maybelle's guitar; Jimmie Rodgers's Texas prairie soul and bad boy sophistication; and the yodel that the next two generations of country singers would grow up imitating. Most of all, the Carters and Jimmie Rodgers sang songs that reflected the passions and perspectives of working-class rural adults. They sang in voices that country people knew belonged to them.

Neither Jimmie Rodgers nor the original Carter Family had long careers. But in a little over a decade, they laid the foundations for all the country music to come. Through the songs they recorded, and the powerful influence they had on the first country fans, their impact on the music continues unabated. When today's alt country artists reach for a rustic, hard-edged sound, and when the stars of the *Grand Ole Opry* gather on stage for a sing-along, it's probably a Carter Family or Jimmie Rodgers song they're singing.

Q In search of more hillbilly music, Victor sent producer Ralph Peer on a tour of the South that included a little town straddling the Tennessee-Virginia border. What was the name of the town? And can you name two of the acts he discovered there?

A Peer's stay in the town of Bristol in July 1927 is just one of hundreds of similar excursions made by record company talent scouts in the early days of commercial recording, but this one has become legendary because of the gold mine of music it unearthed. During the famous "Bristol Sessions," Peer made recordings of the two acts who would go on to dominate country music over the next two decades: Jimmie Rodgers and the Carter Family.

Q What's the name of the man born in Maces Springs, Virginia, who created perhaps the greatest and most beloved country vocal group of all time?

A Alvin Pleasant Delaney Carter, born December 15, 1891, would become known to history as A.P. Carter, founder of the Carter Family. He was the driving force behind the group's commercial success, and the man who copyrighted dozens of songs that became the foundation of the country music songbook.

Q What is the name of the region in which Maces Springs is located?

A Poor Valley, an appropriate enough name for a place that exemplified the hard-scrabble farming existence of the southern Appalachians.

When A.P.'s mother was eight months pregnant with him, she was nearly struck by a bolt of lightning. What characteristic of her son did she attribute to that incident?

A.P.'s physical and vocal tremor, which lasted his entire life. His hands shook so badly that he could hardly write; along with his nervous energy and sensitive nature, the affliction made him poorly suited for school or farm work. He embraced music as his consolation, and when he matured the tremor gave him a distinctive singing voice.

A.P. tried working on the railroad, and when that failed he took up selling fruit trees. He was trying to sell one at his aunt's house one day when he encountered a woman sitting beneath a tree, strumming an autoharp and singing "Engine 143." Who was she?

A.P.'s future wife, Sara Dougherty, who, as Sara Carter, would become country music's first female singing star. Orphaned before she was five years old, Sara had a barely subdued pain in her voice that struck everyone who heard her sing. A.P. was smitten instantly; it took Sara longer to come around, but she later said that she gradually fell in love with him because of his singing voice. They married in 1915, and the couple became sought after to play and sing at church gatherings.

Who was the third member of the Carter Family? And how did she come by her last name?

The first of the great country guitar players was born Maybelle Addington in Nickelsville, Virginia, in 1909. A cousin of Sara's, she went on to marry A.P.'s brother, Ezra Carter. Maybelle started playing guitar at age 12, and began to perform with A.P. and Sara in 1927, just before their Victor audition.

Were the Carter Family's Bristol Session recordings the first they had made?

No; they had auditioned earlier in 1927 for Brunswick in Norton, Virginia. But Brunswick wanted to cast A.P. as a country fiddler, and A.P. wanted to sing; as a result, the Carters turned the record company's offer down. The fact that back-porch musicians from Poor Valley had two chances to audition for major labels within a year demonstrates how diligently the record companies were searching for hillbilly talent.

Identify the song:
Well my heart is sad/And I am lonesome
For the only one I love
When shall I meet him?/Oh, no, never
Till we meet in heaven above...

"Bury Me Beneath the Weeping Willow," the first song recorded by the Carter Family for Victor. Between 1927 and 1943, the group would record more than 300 songs, many of which would go on to become the foundation of the country music repertoire.

The Carters were unlike most hillbilly acts in one very important respect. What was it?

Their clothes. By the time the Carters recorded, it was already conventional for old timey music acts to dress up in some kind of costume, usually a send up of either the hillbilly or cowboy motif. The Carters, by contrast, always dressed in their Sunday-go-to-meeting best, the better to portray an image of wholesome respectability.

A.P. Carter copyrighted hundreds of songs in his lifetime. How many did he actually write?

It's hard to tell for sure, but probably not more than a relative handful of them. Most of A.P.'s "compositions" were songs he gathered, first from friends and neighbors, and then on extended automobile expeditions throughout the South in search of songs, collecting old sheet music and gospel hymnals. A.P. readily admitted that most of the songs copyrighted in his name were from traditional sources.

If A.P. didn't write most of the Carter Family's songs, why did he copyright them in his own name?

His producer, Ralph Peer, insisted on it. While records might sell well, publishing was where the big money was made in the music industry. The practice of protecting "arrangements" of traditional songs was already well established; with the Carter Family's music protected under A.P.'s name, Peer could publish the songs through his own company, Southern Music. He split the publishing profits with A.P. Although the practice might seem dubious, many old songs that may have otherwise been forgotten were preserved thanks to A.P. Carter's song-hunting expeditions.

In 1928, the Carters traveled to Camden, New Jersey, to record. The session produced a wealth of songs that would become country standards, including "Wildwood Flower," "Keep on the Sunny Side," and "Will the Circle be Unbroken." How much were the group paid for this historic recording session?

$50. They also signed a contract that paid them a modest royalty on record and sheet music sales.

Who invented the guitar picking method known as the "Carter Scratch"?

Maybelle is often credited with creating the style, in which the thumb picks out the melody line on the bass strings while the fingers strum an accompaniment; but in fact she may have learned it from Leslie Riddle, a black guitarist who became a friend of A.P. and who joined him on many of his music hunting excursions.

The Carter Family classic, "I'm Thinking Tonight of My Blue Eyes," has something important in common with two later country hits, Roy Acuff's "Great Speckled Bird," and Kitty Wells's "It Wasn't God Who Made Honky Tonk Angels." What is it?

All three songs (and many others besides) have the same melody.

How many million-selling records did the Carter Family record?

None. While many of their records did well by the standards of the day, the group never had a real hit record; by 1930, their total record sales were only 700,000. Their audience wasn't large, but it was faithful, and it grew with each new generation.

In 1932, when she wasn't traveling the country singing songs in praise of religion and down-home values, what was Sara Carter doing?

Having an affair with A.P.'s cousin, Coy Bays. A.P.'s frequent absences in search of songs left Sara with plenty of time on her hands, and his nasty temper provided the motivation to look elsewhere for affection. By 1936, Sara's marriage to A.P. Carter was finished.

Did Sara's breakup with A.P. mean an end to the Carter Family?

No; in fact, the Carter Family continued to portray the image of a happy hillbilly family until 1943, when Sara finally quit the group for good.

In 1938, the Carters moved to Texas. Why?

To take advantage of the phenomenon of "border radio."
In the United States, the signal power of radio transmitters
was restricted to avoid interference, so stations could only be
heard within a limited radius. In Mexico, no such limitations
existed, and broadcasters set up huge transmitters just across
the border that could reach virtually the entire U.S. audience.
Thanks to border radio, country music could be heard in
every nook and cranny of America.

By 1939, three more Carters were singing with the group.
Who were they?

Maybelle's three daughters, Helen, June, and Anita. Later,
following the breakup of the original Carter Family, Maybelle
continued performing with her daughters as "Mother Maybelle
and the Carter Sisters." June Carter would go on to a successful
solo career and to record hit duets with her second husband,
Johnny Cash.

What act of the federal government virtually ended the Carter Family?

In 1941, the United States signed a broadcasting treaty with Mexico that essentially put the border radio stations out of business. The Carters' sponsor moved their show to a local station in Charlotte, North Carolina, for a couple of seasons; but when their contract ran out in 1943, Sara, fed up with having to travel from California to perform with the group, made a permanent break.

The week of December 7, 1941, *Life* magazine was scheduled to run a big feature article about the Carter Family, but it never appeared. Why not?

It was bumped by a bigger story: the Japanese bombing of Pearl Harbor that ushered the United States into World War II.

Was Sara's departure the end of the Carter Family story?

The act may have been history, but the legend had just begun. Mother Maybelle and the Carter Sisters could still be heard performing Carter Family music on the radio, including their appearances on the *Grand Ole Opry*. And when Harry Smith included several old Carter Family recordings on his seminal collection, *The Anthology of American Folk Music*, in 1953, he bequeathed the Carters' sound to the generation that founded the Folk Revival. Every budding guitarist learned Maybelle's finger-picking figures on "Wildwood Flower," and folk groups like the Kingston Trio had big hits with Carter Family songs.

In 1967, Sara and Maybelle reunited for a performance. What was the name of the premier roots music festival they headlined?

The Newport Folk Festival.

Why didn't A.P. Carter join Sara and Maybelle on stage at Newport?

He was dead. A.P. Carter died back where he started, in Maces Springs, in 1960.

The Country Music Hall of Fame was founded in 1961; Jimmie Rodgers was its first inductee. When was the Carter Family inducted?

Not until 1970.

They still play old time music in Maces Springs every Saturday night. What's the name of the venue that promotes Carter Family music there?

The Carter Fold, founded by A.P. and Sara's daughter, Janette, in 1974. Bring the family; no liquor or smoking allowed. At the nearby Carter Family Museum, you can see the little cabin where A.P. was born.

The other big find Ralph Peer made at the 1927 Bristol Sessions was the first country music superstar, Jimmie Rodgers. What were Rodgers's two nicknames, and how did he come by them?

 Thanks to his penchant for bluesy melodies and his habit of punctuating the verses of his songs with a lilting yodel, he was billed as "The Blue Yodeler." And by working the railroad mystique into his compositions, he also became known as "The Singing Brakeman."

 Was Jimmie Rodgers actually ever a brakeman?

 He was indeed. Born in 1897 in Meridian, Mississippi, the young Jimmie loved to entertain, and by 13 he was already organizing traveling shows. Partly to keep him home, Jimmie's father got him his first job as a water boy on the railroad. He later went on to become a brakeman on the New Orleans and Northeastern line. It was as a railroad man that he encountered the hoboes and rounders who were the subjects of so many of his songs—and the bluesy singing of black railroad workers, which he made the hallmark of his style.

What ended Jimmie Rodgers's railroad career?

Tuberculosis. Jimmie was only 27 when he contracted the disease in 1924; thanks to the coughing and fatigue characteristic of tuberculosis, by 1927 his days as a railroad man were over. Rodgers turned to music, not only because he loved entertaining, but as a non-strenuous way to make a living.

Identify the song:
It's T for Texas, T for Tennessee
T for Texas, T for Tennessee
And it's T for Thelma
That woman who made a big fool out of me

The lyrics are from "Blue Yodel," Jimmie Rodgers's first big hit. After the test recordings Rodgers made for Peer in Bristol did reasonably well, Rodgers went to New York and convinced Victor to let him cut some more. "Blue Yodel" (later known as "Blue Yodel No. 1") was Jimmie Rodgers's breakthrough hit, selling nearly a half-million copies over the next two years.

Name the song that contains the lines, *I'm goin' to California, where they sleep out every night/I'm leavin' you mama, because you know you don't treat me right.*

"Blue Yodel No. 4"

And the song with the lines, *Listen all you rounders, you'd better leave my women alone/or I'll take my special and run all you rounders home?*

 That would be "Blue Yodel No. 9."

 While we're on "Blue Yodel No. 9," what distinctive instrumentation did the song feature, and who was responsible for it?

 The recording showcases one of the few jazz cornets you'll ever hear on a country record. It was played by none other than the master, Louis Armstrong. The song was recorded in Los Angeles in 1930.

 Identify the song:
I went up to a brakeman
To give him a line of talk
He said "If you've got money
I'll see that you don't walk."
I hadn't got a nickel
Not a penny could I show.
"Get off, get off, you railroad bum!"
And he slammed the boxcar door.

 They're the lyrics from Jimmy Rodgers's best-known song, "Waiting for a Train," recorded in 1928.

Identify the song:
When it rained down sorrow it rained all over me
When it rained down sorrow it rained all over me
'Cause my body rattles like a train on that old SP...

"T.B. Blues," recorded in 1931, one of two songs Rodgers recorded about the struggle with tuberculosis.

Did Jimmie Rodgers perform in the hillbilly getup typical of other country acts?

Far from it. He did pose for publicity photos in cowboy and railroad costumes, but on stage and on the street he liked to flaunt his money, wearing fancy suits, jewelry, and a jauntily cocked straw hat.

How else did Jimmie Rodgers's stage persona differ from other country acts of the day?

Unlike the mix of sentimental morality and hillbilly high jinks that were standard fare for old-time music performers, Rodgers projected an image of worldly wise sophistication. He did his share of tender ballads about mother and home, and even recorded a few religious numbers; but the songs he's remembered for portray the hard and fast life of drinking, gambling, prostitution, grifting, and drifting. While the Carter Family advertised their music as "morally good," Jimmie Rodgers was country music's original bad boy, a persona that would be nearly as influential with future stars as his yodel.

After the style of blues musicians, Jimmie Rodgers would often call out various phrases during the instrumentals of his songs. Can you recite any?

There were lots of them, but the most frequent were probably these:
"Hey, hey!"
"Go to town!"
"Man, man!"
"It won't be long now . . ."
"Play that thing, boy!"

After the Bristol Sessions, how long did Jimmie Rodgers's music career last?

Barely six years. He recorded and performed constantly between 1928 and his death in 1933; his popularity was so great that he even made a short film for Columbia Pictures. By the time he was 35, tuberculosis was taking a greater and greater toll on his energy; he had to sit down to perform. On May 26, 1933, he died; but the 110 songs he recorded went on to become classics, inspiring many of the country music stars who emerged in the 1930s and 1940s.

By 1930, Jimmie Rodgers and the Carter Family were the preeminent stars of country music. Did they ever record together?

They did; in 1931, they got together in Louisville to record two novelty numbers: *Jimmie Rodgers Visits the Carter Family,* and *The Carter Family and Jimmie Rodgers in Texas.*

What do Gene Autry, Lefty Frizzell, Ernest Tubb, and Hank Snow have in common, besides being among the pantheon of country music's greatest stars?

They were all huge Jimmie Rodgers fans, who credited the Blue Yodeler with igniting their interest in country music, and who spent their early careers trying to imitate him.

Roy Acuff may have looked hillbilly, but his star power and music-publishing empire helped make country music an industry. Here's Roy singing with the Smoky Mountain Boys at the Opry.

CHAPTER THREE

Hillbillies in High Cotton

The phonograph and the radio had a number of curious effects on country music. To begin with, of course, they brought hillbillies out of the hills and made their music available, not only to other country folk but to people in towns and cities throughout North America. But even as the new media fed the desire of a growing audience to listen to "old-timey" music, the commercial pressures it brought to bear on that music changed it in profound ways. There were no longer any isolated regions for unique music to develop. At the same time, the hillbilly image projected to the mass market often had more to do with the fantasies of northern music promoters and record producers than with any genuine expression of backwoods culture.

And as a growing number of stars demonstrated their ability to be hugely successful commercially, the pressure to smooth the rough edges off the music and conform to proven marketing formulas became harder to resist. Youngsters in the 1930s learned songs, not only from family and neighbors, but increasingly from the professionals they heard on records and broadcasts, and those were the models they imitated as they dreamed of being stars themselves.

Singers like Dock Boggs and A.P. Carter may have been the pioneers of country music, but it's clear they would have stood little chance in the Nashville star system that prevailed by the end of the 1940s. Radio and records created "country music" as an industry, and at the same time, extinguished it as a genuine folk music form.

Bascom Lamar Lunsford is remembered for preserving the folk music of the Appalachians, having founded the Mountain Dance and Folk Festival in Asheville, North Carolina in 1928. A fiddler and banjo player, he recorded more than 300 songs and stories for academic institutions like the Library of Congress, but he wrote and recorded a few commercial sides as well. Can you name the most famous of them?

He wrote the country standard, "Mountain Dew," which he sold to the novelty duo, Lulu Belle and Scotty, in 1928 for $25.

Another folk archivist, famous for his rendition of the ballad "Barbara Allen," was one of the early stars of the *National Barn Dance*. Name him.

Bradley Kincaid, born in Point Leavell, Kentucky, in 1895. The young Kincaid became involved in the YMCA movement, which emphasized folk singing and dancing as a form of moral improvement. While attending the YMCA college in Chicago, he joined a vocal quartet that was performing on WLS; when station managers learned about his storehouse of mountain songs, they let him perform solo on the *Barn Dance* program. His traditional folk songs were an immediate success, and Kincaid was a regular on the program for three years, before going on to a string of other radio gigs around the country and eventually ending up on the *Grand Ole Opry* in the late 1940s.

Besides helping to popularize mountain music on the radio, what other distinction does Bradley Kincaid hold?

He was the first country radio star to publish a songbook. WLS was owned by Sears, Roebuck and Co.; as Kincaid's popularity grew, you could buy his *Favorite Mountain Ballads and Old Time Songs* in the Sears catalog. The 1928 songbook sold more than 100,000 copies; thanks to its simple arrangements, amateur musicians around the country were playing songs that had seldom been heard outside the Smoky Mountains a few years before.

Name the act that was the anchor string band on the *Grand Ole Opry* in 1928 and recorded at Victor Records' very first Nashville recording session.

The Gully Jumpers, featuring Paul Warmack on mandolin, C.B. Arrington on fiddle, William Roy Hardison on banjo, and Burt Hutcherson on guitar. All were Nashville-area locals who maintained their day jobs when they weren't performing. The Gully Jumpers were perennial *Opry* favorites for decades, and appeared on the show in various formations right up to the 1970s.

Gid Tanner was just a Georgia chicken farmer who could play a little fiddle, but he went on to found one of the most popular of the early country string bands. Who were they?

The Skillet Lickers. Gid may not have been a violin virtuoso, but he knew what audiences liked, and the Skillet Lickers combined sprightly dance music with wacky onstage antics. They were regulars on the *Opry*, and their 1934 RCA Victor hit, "Down Yonder," sold a million copies.

Name the other local string band with a goofy name that signed off the *Opry* broadcasts in the 1930s.

The Fruit Jar Drinkers, composed of West Nashville boys George Wilkerson on fiddle, Tommy Leffew on mandolin, and Howard Ragsdale on guitar. Although they were one of the foundations of the early *Opry*, they made no commercial recordings.

Who cooked up the cornpone names of the *Opry* string bands?

George D. Hay, who wanted to play the hillbilly angle to the hilt. For example, he changed the name of Dr. Bate's Augmented String Orchestra to the Possum Hunters.

Although George D. Hay continued to perform the announcer duties on the *Opry* for years to come, by 1932 he was no longer WSM's program director. What happened?

Hay may have been a genius as a showman, but he wasn't much of a manager. Hay's increasing health problems often kept him out of the office as well. WSM's affairs were in such a mess that Hay was replaced as program director and relegated mostly to doing publicity and announcing.

Who replaced Hay at the helm of WSM?

Harry Stone, initially hired as an announcer at WSM, was promoted to program director in 1932. The son of a Florida Coca-Cola bottling plant operator who moved to Nashville, he began experimenting with radio broadcasting in the early 1920s. He ran two small Nashville radio stations before joining WSM in 1928.

What two major innovations did Harry Stone bring to the *Grand Ole Opry?*

First of all, in an attempt to attract more sponsors to the show, he divided the program up into half-hour segments, each with its own advertising sponsor. The format stuck, and was copied by many other hayride and barn dance radio shows. More importantly for the evolution of country music, he ended Hay's reliance on local string bands and focused instead on building a stable of star vocalists. As a result, the Opry became the place that the careers of many of the country stars of the 1940s were launched, and vocalists replaced string bands as the staple of country music.

As the live audience for the *Opry* began to grow, the show had to move its location to accommodate the crowds. Can you trace the movement of the *Grand Ole Opry?*

The show began in the offices of the National Life and Accident Insurance Company. In 1928, a new home, dubbed Studio B, was built for the show; it seated an audience of 200. The show moved twice in 1934, first to an even larger Studio B, then to the Hillsboro Theatre. Another move was required in 1936, taking the show to the Dixie Tabernacle until 1939, when it moved to the War Memorial Auditorium in downtown Nashville. In 1943, the *Opry* moved to the Ryman Auditorium, where it remained for the next 31 years before moving to the Opryland theme park in 1974.

Name the fiddle player from Maynardville, Tennessee, whose soulful voice helped him become the first big star of the *Grand Ole Opry?*

It was none other than Roy Claxton Acuff, born in 1903, who cut his first records in 1936 and played the *Opry* for the first time in 1937. While he was firmly in the *Opry's* mountain string band tradition, his expressive singing style made him stand out. Roy Acuff was therefore an important transition figure in the *Opry's* star system and, by extension, the growing dominance of individual singing stars in country music.

What were the two songs that propelled Acuff to superstardom?

"Great Speckled Bird," which Acuff premiered on the *Opry* in 1938; and his signature hit, "Wabash Cannon Ball," which he sang on the show continually until his death in 1992.

What was Roy Acuff before he became a professional musician?

An athlete. He played semi-professional baseball, and also boxed; in 1929, he was recruited by the New York Yankees. Unfortunately, an earlier bout with sunstroke caused Roy to collapse during a game; a nervous breakdown followed in 1930, and his sports career was over.

To what did Roy Acuff turn to help in his recuperation?

His fiddle, which he'd learned to play as a child. He got the performing bug, and started playing with a traveling medicine show in 1932. Local radio performances in Knoxville followed, and he was invited to record for the American Radio Corporation. A 1936 Chicago session included recordings of "Great Speckled Bird" and "Wabash Cannon Ball."

"Great Speckled Bird" is an allegorical song about the Christian church. On what Bible verse is it based?

Jeremiah 12:9, which reads, "Mine heritage is unto me as a speckled bird, the birds round about are against her; come ye, assemble all the beasts of the field, come to devour."

Finish the verse:
Oh the Eastern states are dandy, so the Western people say
From New York to St. Louis and Chicago by the way
To the hills of Minnesota where the rippling waters fall . . .

No changes can be taken on the Wabash Cannonball.
The folk song, of unknown origin, was originally recorded by the Carter Family in 1929.

With an itinerary that spans the entire United States, that Wabash Cannonball is some train. Was there ever a real Wabash Cannonball?

 You get the point whether you answered yes or no. At the time Acuff recorded the song, it was entirely fictional; but after the song became a hit, the Wabash Railroad named the train on its Detroit to St. Louis line after the mythical rattler. The Wabash Cannonball was also the name of a roller coaster at Opryland USA.

 What was the name of Roy Acuff's string band?

 They originally recorded under the name "The Crazy Tennesseans," but a WSM executive suggested the change to "The Smoky Mountain Boys."

 The expressive Dobro work of Beecher Ray Kirby was a distinctive part of the Roy Acuff sound, and helped make the steel guitar a must-have element of country music. By what stage name is Kirby better known? And how did he acquire it?

 When the Smoky Mountain Boys acquired an unmarried female singer and banjo player, Acuff's concern about conservative country sensibilities led him to create the fiction that she had a brother in the band who served as her escort. He dubbed Kirby "Bashful Brother Oswald," the name by which we remember him.

While we're on it, what exactly is a Dobro?

Originally a specific brand of resonator guitar, the term is often applied today to any resonator. As the guitar became more popular as a band instrument, its soft tone was a problem in the days before electric amplification. The resonator was an early solution; a metal cone was built into the heart of the guitar, and its resonance would create a louder sound that could be heard over a band—or the noise of a crowded tavern.

According to the lyrics of another Roy Acuff hit, "The Wreck on the Highway," what two fluids mingle to create a grisly cocktail?

Whiskey and blood:
There was whiskey and blood all together
Mixed with glass where they lay
Death played her hand in destruction
But I didn't hear nobody pray.

What 1939 event propelled Roy Acuff to national stardom?

The NBC radio network began broadcasting a half-hour of the *Grand Ole Opry* nationwide as the *Prince Albert Show*.

Roy Acuff's records, songbooks, and personal appearances made him a fairly wealthy man by 1942. But his greatest riches lay ahead of him. What business did he go into?

He joined up with songwriter Fred Rose to form Acuff-Rose Publications. Acuff-Rose went on to publish the songs of such stars as Bob Wills, Eddie Arnold, and Hank Williams, and became the first music publishing powerhouse in Nashville.

One of the early products of the Nashville star system was a music student from Georgetown College who got his stage name from the color of his hair. Name him.

Clyde Julian Foley, known to country fans as Red Foley. He started off on the *National Barn Dance* in 1931, and was a regular on a number of other barn dance radio programs before becoming a regular headliner on the *Grand Ole Opry* in 1946. He continued to MC the nationally broadcast *Opry* segment until 1953, and continued recording and touring until his death in 1968. His most commercially successful record was his 1950 hit, "Chattanoogie Shoe Shine Boy."

Finish the verse:
. . . if dogs have a heaven
There's one thing I know . . .

. . . Old Shep has a wonderful home.
A sentimental ballad about putting down man's best friend, "Old Shep" was penned by Foley, and became his first break-through hit record in 1941.

Four years later, a ten-year-old boy sang "Old Shep" as his performance in the Alabama State Fair talent contest, and it was good enough for second prize. What was the boy's name?

Elvis Presley, who later recorded the song as an adult. Many artists have covered "Old Shep," including Hank Snow.

Red Foley often included gospel numbers in his repertoire, and one of his greatest hits is a sacred song he recorded with The Sunshine Boys in 1951. What was the song, and for whom was it originally written?

Thomas A. Dorsey, "The Father of Gospel Music," wrote "Peace in the Valley" for the great Mahalia Jackson in 1939.

He was born Julius Frank Anthony Kuczynski in Milwaukee, Wisconsin, in 1914, and grew up playing polkas on his accordion. By what name do country fans remember him?

Pee Wee King. By the time he was out of high school, he'd gotten the country music bug and began playing on the radio; he appeared on the *Badger State Barn Dance* in 1933 and had his own show on Racine's WJRN. He headed for Dixie in 1936, and became Gene Autry's accordionist. In 1937, he formed the Golden West Cowboys and began a ten-year run on the *Grand Ole Opry*.

Name the two major innovations Pee Wee King introduced to country music.

 First was his instrumentation: along with the traditional country instruments, King added horns, drums, and electric guitars, in general producing a bigger and more polished sound that would be a major influence on the honky-tonk acts to come. The second was his clothes. Eschewing the backwoods getups that had been standard on the *Opry*, King dressed his band in fancy cowboy outfits created by Hollywood fashion designer, Nudie Cohn. The style caught on, and appearing in a custom-made "Nudie suit" became a sure sign that you had arrived in country music. King was also one of the first country performers on TV, including the *Pee Wee King Show* on ABC.

He started out in Ravia, Oklahoma, trying to imitate his hero Jimmie Rodgers on a Sears mail-order guitar. By 1934, however, he had created a new performance genre that would have a powerful impact on country music. Who was he?

Ovron Grover Autry, who became Gene Autry, the first of the great singing cowboys. Born in 1907 in Tioga, Texas, the Autry family moved to Oklahoma in 1920. Inspired by a chance meeting with humorist Will Rodgers, Autry went to New York in 1927 to make test recordings of pop songs for Victor and Edison. When he failed to get a contract, he went to Tulsa and got a radio job as "Oklahoma's Yodeling Cowboy," and later joined the cast of the *National Barn Dance*. Cowboy movie stars like Tom Mix and Buck Jones were popular, and Autry continued burnishing his western image, recording a mix of Jimmie Rodgers songs and cowboy numbers like "The Last Roundup" and "Cowboy's Heaven." In 1934 he went to California to make a cameo appearance in the Ken Maynard film, *In Old Santa Fe*. Soon he was starring in his own pictures, and between films, records, and the radio, became one of America's most popular entertainers, creating a mythical frontier where virtuous cowboys sang lilting melodies while playing guitar on horseback.

Finish the verse:
If God would but grant me the power
To turn back the pages of time
I'd give all I own, if I could but atone . . .

. . . to that silver-haired daddy of mine.
The sentimental classic, "That Silver-Haired Daddy of Mine," was Autry's first big hit record in 1932.

What was the name of Gene Autry's first movie serial?

 The Phantom Empire, a 12-part series released in 1935 that answers the question, "If science fiction movies and cowboy movies are both popular, wouldn't a cowboy science fiction movie be even better?" Gene's ranch is attacked by robots (apparently made out of oil barrels) from the techno-savvy underground empire of Murania. Truly one of the strangest Saturday serials ever made, but it certainly didn't hurt Autry's movie career.

 What was the name of Gene Autry's horse?

 Champion.

 According to Autry's 1939 hit, "Back in the Saddle Again," upon what do the longhorn cattle feed?

 The lowly gypsum weed. Given that *Datura stramonium* contains hallucinogenic alkaloids, it's probably better not to let the cattle eat too much of it.

What was the name of Gene Autry's CBS radio show between 1940 and 1956?

Gene Autry's Melody Ranch.

Hammurabi had his code; Moses had his Ten Commandments. What was Gene Autry's contribution to the literature of public morality?

The Cowboy Code, which coincidentally also had ten commandments, designed to instill true western virtues in Autry's youthful radio audience. Along with helping people in distress and always telling the truth, the Code admonished cowboys not to "advocate or possess racially or religiously intolerant ideas," and never to shoot first.

The *Melody Ranch* show was on hiatus between 1942 and 1945. Why?

Gene Autry joined the Army Air Corps to serve in World War II; he actually enlisted on the air during a *Melody Ranch* episode. His military service wasn't show business, however; he flew air transport missions between Burma and China.

As the 1950s wore on, Gene Autry's plain, heartfelt singing style went out of style, and his recording career gradually petered out. But you can still hear a few of his greatest hits on the radio at a special time of year. Can you name some?

 As the singing cowboy bit became old hat, Autry recorded some of the most popular holiday songs of all time, including "Rudolph the Red-Nosed Reindeer," "Here Comes Santa Claus," and "Frosty the Snowman," all million-sellers.

 By 1960, Gene Autry had pretty much given up on his active show business career. What did he do instead?

 He bought a baseball team, the Los Angeles Angels, who later moved to Anaheim. Autry also owned television station KTLA in Los Angeles and a string of radio stations throughout California. He was a very wealthy man when he died of lymphoma at the age of 91 in 1998.

 What unique Hollywood distinction does Gene Autry hold?

 He is the only celebrity to have five stars on the Hollywood Walk of Fame, one each to memorialize his contributions to movies, recording, live performance, radio, and television.

He was an expert on genuine cowboy songs, and had been singing them on the radio since the 1920s. After Gene Autry inaugurated the singing cowboy craze, this singer went to Hollywood to get into the movies himself, and made a string of low-budget westerns for Grand National and Monogram in the 1930s. Who was he?

 Tex Ritter, who made his first movie, *Song of the Gringo,* in 1936.

 A much better movie than *Song of the Gringo* features Tex Ritter, even though he doesn't appear in it. What are we talking about?

 That's Tex singing the narrative soundtrack song in the classic Gary Cooper western, *High Noon.*

 Another act that rode Gene Autry's coattails to Hollywood was certainly the best and most innovative western singing group of all. Who was this group, which began its life as the Pioneer Trio?

 The Sons of the Pioneers, whose tightly-woven block harmonies and sentimental paeans to the lone prairie helped define the western genre. Two of the original members of the group, Tom Nolan and Tim Spencer, penned some of the greatest western songs of all: "Tumbling Tumbleweeds," "Cool Water," "Way Out There," and many more. The group started making radio transcriptions in 1934, and by late in the decade was appearing in the first of many B-western films.

Leonard Franklin Skye was one of the original Sons of the Pioneers, but left the group to become one of the greatest singing cowboys of all. By what name do we know him?

He was actually billed as Leonard Skye in his first B-westerns in 1935 and 1936, including a Gene Autry movie. When Autry walked out on his contract with Republic Pictures, the studio cast Skye in a film in which Autry was supposed to appear, called *Under the Western Stars.* The studio execs changed Skye's name to Roy Rodgers. Rodgers did dozens of westerns up through the early 1950s, had a number of popular cowboy records, and was a star of radio and television as well. He was teamed with actress Dale Evans in the 1944 film, *The Cowboy and the Senorita,* and the two were a team ever after, becoming husband and wife after the death of Rodgers's first wife in 1946.

Jimmie Davis was elected governor of Louisiana in 1942. What had his most notable accomplishment been up to that time?

He was a Victor recording star, one of many yodeling Jimmie Rodgers imitators who made the first hit record with the standard "You Are My Sunshine." Although he's most strongly associated with the sentimental song, he started out recording spicy double-entendre numbers like "Tom Cat and Pussy Blues," "High Behind Blues," and "Do-do-daddling Thing." After his terms as governor, he went on to record gospel music.

What racial contradiction is part of Jimmie Davis's legacy?

That, although he was one of the few white performers to record with black musicians, he ran for governor on a strict segregationist platform.

Name the boys from Elkmont, Alabama who were one of the first of the great brother duos in country music.

Alton and Rabon Delmore, the Delmore Brothers. They learned their plaintive harmonies from their mother, who was a composer of shape-note hymns. They became a hit on the fiddle contest circuit, and joined the *Grand Ole Opry* in 1933; by 1936 they were one of the most popular acts on the show. They left the *Opry* in 1938, but continued performing and recording until the late 1940s.

There were many popular "brother duets" in the 1930s, including Mac & Bob, Karl & Harty, the Monroe Brothers, and the Blue Sky Boys. What did these acts have in common?

If you answered that they were all brothers, you're wrong. Mac & Bob were actually Lester McFarland and Robert Gardner, and Karl & Harty's last names were Davis and Taylor, respectively. No, the real link is their instrumentation—rhythm guitar and lead mandolin. Even though the mandolin had enjoyed an enormous craze in the early years of the 20th century, the brother duets were the first to make it a standard country instrument; and Bill of the Monroe Brothers became the first country mandolin virtuoso.

Ruby Blevins grew up in Hope, Arkansas, the only girl in a family with ten boys. For what distinction is she remembered?

As Patsy Montana, in 1935 she became the first solo female country artist to have a runaway hit, "I Wanna Be a Cowboy's Sweetheart." Her chops as a yodeler and fiddler won her a talent contest in 1931, the prize for which was a job singing on radio. She formed an all-girl western band, the Montana Cowgirls, and performed with other singing cowboy acts. She was discovered by Jimmie Davis, who took her on tour, helping build her reputation. She then joined the Prairie Ramblers, who were regulars on the *National Barn Dance;* when they went to New York to record in 1935, Patsy got a chance to make her signature hit. Her exuberant, independent cowgirl image got her a part in a Gene Autry film and made her a regular on the *Louisiana Hayride* radio show in the 1940s. She continued to perform until her death in 1996.

One of the first great cowboy yodelers to build on the success of Jimmie Rodgers was Montana Slim, a real cowboy and rodeo performer whose hits included "Pete Knight's Last Ride" and "My Little Yoho Lady." Where was Montana Slim born?

His real name was Wilf Carter, and he was born on the lonesome prairies of Nova Scotia, Canada.

What *Opry* star from Rosewood, Kentucky, lends his name to a style of guitar picking?

 Merle Travis, who was the first star of the country electric guitar. Travis learned on a homemade guitar at age 12, hanging around parties and dances to study the unique and infectious two-fingered picking technique several local guitarists used. He went on to perfect the method, in which the thumb plucks out bass lines while the index finger picks the melody lead, now known as "Travis picking."

 Travis was a technical innovator as well as a great guitarist; he was one of the first musicians to experiment with multitrack recording, for instance. His design for a solid-bodied electric guitar inspired a friend of his to design a similar model. Who was this friend?

 Leo Fender, who went on to design the greatest of the early electric guitars, and whose Telecaster model would later come to define the twang of honky tonk.

 In 1946, Travis was asked to record some of the traditional songs he'd learned during his Kentucky boyhood. "Shoot," he said, "I can write better songs than those." What two country standards did he produce to prove his point?

 The coal-mining classics "Sixteen Tons" and "Dark as a Dungeon."

According to the Merle Travis song "Sixteen Tons," why can't a coal miner go to heaven?

 He owes his soul to the company store. "Sixteen Tons" went on to become a hit for both pop singer Frankie Laine and Tennessee Ernie Ford.

 David Akeman was a protégé of Uncle Dave Macon, and became Bill Monroe's first banjo player in 1942. He made many appearances on the *Grand Ole Opry* over the next two decades, and later became one of the most recognized country stars. By what ectomorphic nickname do we know him?

 Thanks to his long, lean frame, his show name became Stringbean. His name became a household word in the 1970s when his comedy was a regular feature on the hit show *Hee Haw.*

 Stringbean made headlines in 1973. How?

He and his wife were brutally murdered in their remote Tennessee cabin by two thieves who were after the cash he was rumored to have hidden there. Twenty-three years later, police found the remnants of hundreds of dollars Stringbean had hidden in the cabin walls.

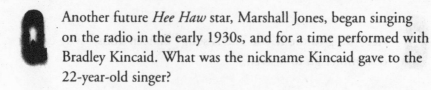 Another future *Hee Haw* star, Marshall Jones, began singing on the radio in the early 1930s, and for a time performed with Bradley Kincaid. What was the nickname Kincaid gave to the 22-year-old singer?

Grandpa Jones, because he sounded like a grumpy old man on the early morning radio program he did with Kincaid. Grandpa Jones learned to play the clawhammer banjo and created a stage getup featuring hillbilly garb and a gray handlebar mustache; he played up the old man shtick for the next sixty years. He went on to join the *Grand Ole Opry* and make hit records like his version of "T for Texas," and gained his greatest recognition after becoming part of the original *Hee Haw* cast in 1967.

From the mid-1940s on, you could often see Grandpa Jones perform with his favorite fiddle player. Who was it?

His wife, Ramona. Their tours with the *Opry* traveling shows and the U.S.O. took them all over the world.

Grandpa Jones formed a gospel quartet, the Brown's Ferry Four, in the early 1940s. Who were the other three members?

Merle Travis, and the Delmore Brothers.

Of what regular *Hee Haw* bit was Grandpa Jones the centerpiece?

"What's for supper, Grandpa?" in which Jones would appear at the kitchen window and recite a rhymed menu featuring stock hillbilly dishes like possum stew and 'tater pie.

What did Grandpa Jones do moments after finishing his *Opry* performance on January 3, 1998?

He suffered a massive stroke; he died a month and a half later.

The king of western swing, Bob Wills.

CHAPTER FOUR

Western Swing and Bluegrass

Two subgenres of country music deserve our attention as we look at the rise of country music in the 1930s and 40s. The first was incubated in the dance halls of the southwest, where musicians took their guitars and fiddles and attempted to incorporate into country music the jazzy sounds of the most popular dance music of the day—swing. The result was western swing, an infectious music that expanded the range and musical sophistication of country without ever losing its Texas twang. While its heyday outside the southwest was brief, it continued to be popular there long after its national decline in the 1950s, and had a tremendous influence on the honky-tonk sound that would dominate country at its popular apex.

The second was a reaction to the increasingly citified sound of country, a return to the simple instrumentations and harmonies of the early hillbilly string bands. But bluegrass was string band music on steroids, demanding a level of musicianship that few back-porch pickers could match. The surging rhythms and high vocal harmonies of bluegrass sounded at once old-timey and yet entirely in keeping with the quickening pace of American life. Like western swing, bluegrass has gone in and out of style since its first appearance in the 1940s, but it seems to enjoy a revival every few years as a new generation of fans discovers the high lonesome sound.

Born in Kosse, Texas, in 1905, he learned to play the fiddle from his daddy and heard the blues and jazz from the many great African-American musicians in East Texas. He would later meld these sounds to create one of the great subgenres of country music. Who was this great band leader, and what is the name of the style he pioneered?

 Jim Rob Wills, known to us as Bob Wills, the creator of the western swing sound. Young Jim Rob's love for the blues cannot be understated; he once rode fifty miles on horseback to hear Bessie Smith sing. Wills played his first barn dance at age 10. He joined a string band called Aladdin's Laddies in 1930, and began integrating the blues and jazz sounds he loved into the old-timey country foundation. His big break came later that year when W. Lee "Pappy" O'Daniel hired the band to promote Light Crust Flour on the radio, and they became the Light Crust Doughboys.

 We need to pause to consider the remarkable career of Pappy O'Daniel, sales manager of the Burrus Mill and Elevator Company in Fort Worth, Texas, which made Light Crust Flour. Besides serving as the announcer on the radio shows that advertised his products, what were O'Daniel's career highlights?

 He served two terms as governor of Texas in 1938 and 1940, and was elected to the U.S. Senate in 1941. O'Daniel knew the power of music, not just to sell flour but to make people feel good about a politician as well, and although he could not sing or play an instrument, his association with the radio string bands that followed him on the campaign trail helped propel him to public office. In the process, he spread the jazzy sound of what would be called western swing throughout the Lone Star State.

Who did Pappy O'Daniel defeat in that 1941 special election to become a senator?

 A greenhorn politician by the name of Lyndon Baines Johnson, who would later become the 36th President of the United States.

 Besides Wills, the lineup of the Light Crust Doughboys contained another future leader of a popular western swing band. Name him.

 Vocalist Milton Brown, who went on to found the Musical Brownies. Unlike Wills's genial trademark sound, Brown followed the jazz muse even further, producing a hot style ideal for dancing. The Brownies were the first act to feature an electric steel guitar, and their stylistic innovation of pairing violin and steel guitar lead solos was widely copied by other western swing acts, including Wills.

After Milton Brown left the Doughboys, Wills was right behind him, and along with fellow Doughboy Tommy Duncan, formed his own western swing band. What was it called?

 The Texas Playboys. After rambling around the southwest for a while, the Playboys landed a daily program on Tulsa's powerful station KVOO in 1934, and Wills's popularity began to take off. He added brass, reeds, drums, and steel guitar to his ensemble, and began featuring the full-bodied kind of arrangements the early big bands were making popular—but with a distinctive Texas drawl. Bob Wills & The Texas Playboys began recording a string of hit records in 1935, and country music would never be the same.

 Did Milton Brown's band provide much competition for the Texas Playboys?

 It might have, and the sound of western swing might have evolved much differently, if Milton Brown had not died in 1936 as a result of injuries he sustained in a car accident.

Bob Wills didn't do much lead singing with the Texas Playboys, and he usually left the lead fiddle role to others. Yet on every recording, he's at the heart of the Playboys' sound. How?

He may not have taken the lead vocal, but he was vocalizing constantly, calling out the names of the soloists, making wry comments on the lyrics of songs, yodeling an improvised fragment of melody, or interjecting trademark exclamations like "yes, yes" and the falsetto sing-song "awwww, now!" It was a practice he probably picked up from jazz stars like Fats Waller, but Wills made it an art form, and it was imitated in one form or another by many country acts.

Finish the verse:
Lonesome song, empty words, I know,
Still live in my heart all alone
For that moonlit path by the Alamo . . .

. . . and Rose, my Rose of San Antone.
"San Antonio Rose," written by Wills in 1940, was the Texas Playboys' biggest hit and sold millions of copies. It became a country standard, covered by everyone from Patsy Cline to Elvis Presley to John Denver.

According to the Bob Wills song "Maiden's Prayer," what does every word of her prayer reveal?

Every word reveals an empty, broken heart/Broken by fate that holds them so far apart.

Finish the verse:
Little bee sucks the blossom, big bee gets the honey . . .

. . . *Darkie picks the cotton, White man gets the money.*
Lyrics from the Bob Wills song "Take Me Back to Tulsa,"
which he wrote with Tommy Duncan.

The Texas Playboys featured two of the great early steel guitarists of country music. Who were they?

The first was Leon McAuliffe, who followed Wills when he
left the Light Crust Doughboys in 1933. McAuliffe, who
wrote the classic Playboys hit "Steel Guitar Rag," created the
Texas steel guitar sound, combining sprightly melodic lines
with jazz chords that mimicked the horn sections of swing
bands. Wills's cry, "Take it away, Leon!" is a hallmark of many
of the Playboys' hits from the 1930s. When McAuliffe left
the band following World War II, he was replaced by Herb
Remington, an acolyte of Hawaiian music who didn't know
much country material when he joined the Playboys. He
learned quickly however, and wrote Wills's 1949 hit, "Boot
Heel Drag."

After World War II, Wills and the band moved to San Francisco, where they did a syndicated radio program from the Fairmont Hotel. Under what name can you buy the recordings of that show today?

 They came to be known as the *Tiffany Transcriptions.* They are prized by Bob Wills fans because they feature long-form arrangements that Wills was unable to record commercially due to the three-minute time limit of 78-rpm records.

 Even though the big band sound was in eclipse by 1950, the Texas Playboys retained a strong following. What was the name of the ballad Wills wrote that became a top ten hit in that year?

 "Faded Love." While the rest of the music world was changing dramatically around him, Wills continued to play the music he innovated, and even continued touring with house bands after he disbanded the Texas Playboys in 1967. A debilitating stroke ended his active performing career in 1969.

 By the 1970s, the resurging interest in classic country music created a western swing revival. Was Bob Wills able to take advantage of it?

 He had enough left in him to record one last album, *For the Last Time,* in 1973. From his wheelchair, he directed a band featuring several of the great Playboys musicians, including Leon McAuliffe and Eldon Shamblin. Immediately after the recording sessions, he suffered another stroke, slipped into a coma, and never recovered consciousness. Bob Wills eventually died of pneumonia in 1975.

Another musician on Bob Wills's last album was never a Texas Playboy, but he was a huge fan who was already making his own mark on country music. What was his name?

 Merle Haggard, who had loved western swing since childhood, recorded a number of Bob Wills numbers, and often incorporated elements of the Texas Playboys sound in his music. Wills's influence can also be heard in the music of Buck Owens and Willie Nelson.

 Another bandleader to come out of the southwest is largely forgotten now, but he was a key figure in bringing western swing to California—in fact, he's the first musician to popularize the phrase. Name this fiddle player who was born in Grand, Oklahoma in 1910.

 Spade Cooley, who was an accomplished fiddler by the time he was a teenager and began playing with Oklahoma dance bands. When the Depression hit, he joined the wave of westward-bound Okies and ended up in California, where he managed to get work playing extra and stand-in parts in the movies and playing with various bands. A promoter was impressed with him and set him up as a bandleader at the Venice Pier Ballroom in Los Angeles in 1942. The big swing orchestra he put together was an immediate hit, and Spade Cooley went on to record several top ten hits and to appear on radio and in B-movies into the 1950s.

What was Spade Cooley's first hit?

"Shame on You," which spent nine weeks at the #1 spot in 1945.

Spade Cooley worked with a number of great musicians, including a steel guitarist who is considered by many today to be the greatest of the western swing steel players. What was the romantic-sounding name Cooley gave to guitarist Earl Murphey?

Joaquin. Joaquin Murphey was a true steel guitar virtuoso, combining pyrotechnic melodic lines with jazz chords no other steel player had ever dreamed of. His instrumental work on recordings like "Three Way Boogie," "Oklahoma Stomp," and "Honeysuckle Rose" became legendary, and had a tremendous influence on the generation of steel players who would make the instrument the cornerstone of the honky-tonk sound.

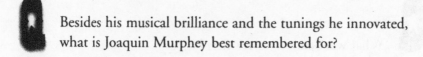

Q Besides his musical brilliance and the tunings he innovated, what is Joaquin Murphey best remembered for?

A His bizarre behavior. He'd walk off stage if things weren't to his liking, de-tune his guitar so no one would learn his tunings behind his back, and was once seen laying in the street talking to his car. Murphey resisted touring, and when the decline of western swing and the non-pedal steel guitar occurred at the end of the 1950s, he slipped into obscurity. He managed to make a few more recordings during the last years of his life, and died in 1999.

Q Spade Cooley's popularity also declined after the western swing craze faded, but he made headlines one last time. How?

A In April 1961, he tortured and murdered his wife, Ella Mae, at his Kern County ranch, with his fourteen-year-old daughter looking on. Cooley was convicted of first-degree murder and sent to prison for the rest of his life.

Q How did Spade Cooley die?

A He was given a furlough from prison in November 1969 to perform at a police benefit concert. After receiving a standing ovation, he walked off stage, suffered a massive heart attack, and died a few weeks before his 59th birthday.

One of the musicians who was part of Red Foley's band was fascinated as a boy by the Hawaiian steel guitar when a traveling tent show came to his home town of Lima, Ohio. His work with Foley, and later with Ernest Tubb and Hank Williams, made his steel guitar sound a key element on the *Opry* and in many of country music's most popular recordings. Name this giant among steel guitarists.

It was none other than Jerry Byrd, who started playing lap steel on the radio as a teenager, and played on the *Renfro Valley Barn Dance* before joining Foley's band in 1948. By 1949 he was recording as a solo artist, including his big hit, "Steelin' the Blues" He continued to perform with other country stars and on the *Grand Ole Opry*, but devoted more and more of his effort to Hawaiian music, and was one of the creators of the full-chorded, lush island sound we associate with tiki lounge music.

One of the hallmark elements of Jerry Byrd's style was the tuning he used, one that had already become a standard in western swing music thanks to Leon McAuliffe's work with the Texas Playboys. You're a real country aficionado (or a steel guitar player) if you can name that tuning.

Byrd and McAuliffe tuned their instruments to an open C6th chord. Thanks to the Bob Wills band, C6th is often referred to as the "Texas Tuning" (as opposed to "Nashville Tuning," the E9th chord favored by pedal steel players since the 1960s), but it was Byrd who brought the sound to a wider audience and made it the signature of the country hits of the late 40s and 50s.

What was Joaquin Murphey's opinion of the Nashville Tuning?

He hated it; he thought it was a gimmick that would soon run its course. His refusal to switch to the tuning and to the pedal version of the instrument were among the reasons for his career decline.

By the 1960s, the pedal steel guitar became the dominant voice in country; most steel players adopted the style, but Jerry Byrd never did, preferring to stick to the simpler instrument he'd helped popularize. As a result, Nashville no longer needed him. What did he do?

When country music left Jerry Byrd behind, he left the mainland and moved to Hawaii. There, he got work playing his florid, campy Hawaiian style in the resort hotels, and switched to recording island music exclusively. More importantly, he set up a school to teach steel guitar to Hawaiian young people; the instrument had fallen out of favor, and Byrd's school reintroduced it to a new generation of islanders. From Hawaii to the mainland in the 20s, then from the mainland back to the islands in the 60s and 70s, thanks to Jerry Byrd, the steel guitar had come full circle. He retired in the 1980s, and passed away in 2005.

What is the significance of the plant species *Poa pratensis* to the evolution of country music?

Its common names are smooth meadow-grass and, of course, Kentucky bluegrass. The legendary Bill Monroe, who created the surging string-band sound he would make famous, honored his native Kentucky by naming his band the Blue Grass Boys, thus giving the new music its name.

What makes bluegrass music a distinct subgenre of country?

That's a question country fans can argue over for a good long while. During the bluegrass resurgence that followed Flatt & Scrugg's 1967 hit recording of "Foggy Mountain Breakdown" and Eric Weissberg's even bigger 1972 hit, "Dueling Banjos," most people associated the music with breakneck tempos and precision banjo picking. But when Monroe innovated the form in the 1930s and 40s, it had a softer, gentler sound that fronted the mandolin and fiddle and especially high, close-harmony vocals; that style has found a new generation of fans in the early 21st century. Whatever style you favor, all bluegrass music sticks to the acoustic instrumentation of the hillbilly string band—guitar, fiddle, mandolin, banjo, and bass, with an occasional Dobro thrown in.

What is the phrase used to refer to that special close-harmony singing, and from whence does that style derive?

The style of bluegrass vocalists, who often sing at the very top of their register, is known as the "high lonesome sound." The modal harmonies themselves are vestiges of shape-note singing.

Let·us now praise Bill Monroe, the Father of Bluegrass Music. Where and when was he born?

Rosine, Kentucky, on September 13, 1911. He was the youngest of eight children.

What influence did Pendleton Vandiver have on young Bill?

That would be Bill's fiddle-playing Uncle Pen, from whom the lad learned the sound of old-time string music. When he got old enough, Bill worked local dances with his uncle; the experience is memorialized in the bluegrass classic Bill later wrote:
Late in the evening, about sundown
High in the hills above the town
Uncle Pen played the fiddle—oh, how it would ring!
You could hear it talk, you could hear it sing...

There was a third musician who sometimes worked those dances with Bill and Uncle Pen. Who was he, and what did he contribute to the bluegrass sound?

 It was Arnold Shultz, a black guitarist whose bluesy take on the instrument would become part of Bill Monroe's musical pallet, thus putting the blues in bluegrass.

 Arnold Shultz's two-fingered picking style influenced another country legend we've already discussed. Who and how?

 Shultz's sound was a musical craze in western Kentucky; it was picked up by white musicians, including the young Merle Travis, who would one day give his name to the style.

 Monroe's parents died in 1929, and he followed several of his brothers north to work in the oil refineries of northern Indiana. They didn't leave the music bug behind in the Kentucky hills, however, and soon Bill and brothers Charlie and Birch had a trio together. On what radio show did they begin to appear?

 The *National Barn Dance*, broadcasting from WLS in nearby Chicago.

Besides performing with his brothers on the *Barn Dance*, what did Bill contribute to the show?

He was a square dancer. Square dancing was a big hit on the *Barn Dance*, and later on the *Grand Ole Opry;* callers would sing out the commands to the accompaniment of a string band. The irony of being a dancer on a radio show is softened somewhat when you remember that the programs were produced before large live audiences.

As the demand for their music grew, Bill and Charlie Monroe got the urge to quit their day jobs and pursue a professional career as musicians. Birch, who was the fiddler, decided a music career wasn't for him, and he left the act. What did his departure mean for Bill and Charlie's instrumentation?

That left Charlie on the guitar and Bill on the mandolin; both sang, with Bill contributing high tenor harmonies. The Monroe Brothers became one of the hot mandolin-guitar brother duos of the era, especially after they moved to WBT radio in Charlotte, North Carolina, where their music could be heard all over the Appalachians thanks to WBT's huge transmitter.

What distinguished the Monroe Brothers from the other brother duets?

Speed. Bill Monroe had become a wizard on the mandolin, and liked to show off his chops by playing at full throttle. Audiences used to the gentler rhythms of the old-timey string bands were thrilled by the sheer energy of the Monroe Brothers' surging tempos.

The Monroe Brothers' growing popularity soon gained them a record contract. What was their first hit?

A gospel number, "What Would You Give in Exchange for Your Soul," recorded for RCA in 1936. Gospel songs would always be a mainstay of Bill Monroe's repertoire, and became one of the foundations of bluegrass music as a result.

Finish the verse:
I ain't gonna work on the railroad
And I ain't gonna work on the farm
I'll lay around the shack 'till the mail train comes back . . .

. . . and roll in my sweet baby's arms.
Written by Charlie Monroe, "Roll in My Sweet Baby's Arms" was one of the Monroe Brothers' hits that went on to become a bluegrass standard. In all, the brothers recorded 60 songs for RCA's Bluebird label.

Did success spoil the Monroe Brothers?

Alas, yes. Their brotherly harmony was only vocal; behind the scenes, their fights often came to blows. Soon after their recording career took off, they decided they'd had enough of one another, and split in 1938.

What was Bill's next move?

He put together a band, initially dubbed the Kentuckians; when he moved his operations to Atlanta, however, he changed the name to the Blue Grass Boys.

You're a first-class fool for bluegrass if you can name the lineup of the original Blue Grass Boys.

Cleo Davis picked up Charlie Monroe's old guitar and vocal chores, and Al Wooten played the fiddle. After trying out a jug player, the band switched to string bass, played by Amos Garren. The center of the action was always Bill, however, who switched to lead vocals as well as providing pyrotechnics on the mandolin.

What milestone did Bill Monroe and the Blue Grass Boys achieve in October 1939?

They auditioned for and won a spot on the *Grand Ole Opry,* premiering their hyperactive rendition of the Jimmie Rodgers song, "Mule Skinner Blues." Thanks to WSM's powerful transmitter and NBC syndication, Bill Monroe quickly became a national star. He would be an *Opry* regular for the next four decades.

A pivotal moment in the evolution of bluegrass occurred when two musicians joined the Blue Grass Boys in 1945. Who were they?

The first was singer/guitarist Lester Flatt, who began taking on lead vocals. The second was banjo virtuoso Earl Scruggs, whose rapid-fire, three-finger picking style replaced the more traditional banjo sound of Dave "Stringbean" Akeman. With the addition of Flatt and Scruggs, Monroe now had two other instrumentalists who could match him note for note, and the Blue Grass Boys recordings from the late 1940s are widely acclaimed as having defined the bluegrass genre. Scrugg's precision banjo picking electrified *Opry* audiences, and the five-string banjo would go on to eclipse the mandolin as the signature instrument of bluegrass.

According to the Bill Monroe hit, "Molly and Tenbrooks," how did the racehorse Tenbrooks initially demonstrate his amazing speed?

 Rode all around Memphis, beat the big Memphis train. The race between the Kentucky stud, Ten Broek, and the California filly, Molly McCarty, really happened in 1878, although it's doubtful that Molly was buried afterward "in a coffin ready made." As for Ten Broek's grave, you can visit it in Midway, Kentucky.

 All bluegrass fans know "Molly and Tenbrooks" as a classic in the repertoire, but can you identify the special distinction the song has in the development of bluegrass?

 In 1947, the Stanley Brothers recorded the song, imitating Bill Monroe's style. Others would follow, notably Flatt & Scruggs, who left the Blue Grass Boys to form the Foggy Mountain Boys in 1948. The style of music Bill Monroe created was on its way to becoming a distinct genre of country music.

 According to Bill Monroe's song, "Blue Moon of Kentucky," what do the stars whisper from on high?

 Your love has said goodbye. "Blue Moon of Kentucky" is one of a number of Bill Monroe songs to transcend the bluegrass genre and become a classic of country, rock 'n' roll, and other pop music forms as well.

When did bluegrass music become "bluegrass music"?

Although the genre had been established by the late 40s, it wasn't until the mid-to-late 1950s that people in the music business recognized the need for a name and began using the term. Bill Monroe may have been responsible for the first use of "blue grass" to describe something other than his band (or *Poa pratensis*) when he published his songbook, *Bill Monroe's Blue Grass Country Songs,* in 1950.

Besides the sound and the repertoire, what did Bill Monroe establish for bluegrass music?

The look. No barn dance overalls or flashy Nudie suits for him; Monroe sported a dark business suit and a stylish Stetson cowboy hat. The look expressed both the country roots and musical sophistication of bluegrass, and was imitated by Flatt & Scruggs, the Stanley Brothers, and other early bluegrass acts.

Bill Monroe and bluegrass music had a permanent niche in country music, thanks to shows like the *Grand Ole Opry;* but with the rise of honky tonk and the Nashville Sound, hit bluegrass records were a rarity by the late 50s. However, another pop music trend came along to revive the popularity of the genre in the early 60s. Can you name it?

We call it the Folk Revival, which had emerged from its cult origins on college campuses to become a major force in the music industry. Folk enthusiasts turned away from the slick commercial sound of 50s pop music and went looking for authentic-sounding remnants of America's musical roots. Monroe, Flatt & Scruggs, and other bluegrass pioneers were there to oblige them.

The longest-running annual bluegrass festival started off as the Brown County Jamboree in southern Indiana. By what name do we know it today?

Bean Blossom, for the town that hosts the festival. Bill Monroe had purchased the Jamboree property and used it as a venue for country acts starting in the early 50s. The first one-day bluegrass festivals began in 1960, and in 1967, Monroe organized the first week-long bluegrass festival at the park. He expanded the festival to ten days and added a second festival in the 70s and 80s. Today, Bill Monroe's Bean Blossom Festival is known as "The Granddaddy of Bluegrass Festivals."

How long did Bill Monroe's professional music career last?

About 67 years, if you count from his first gigs with Birch and Charlie. He recorded more than 500 songs during that time, and lived to receive a Heritage Award from the National Endowment for the Arts and a Lifetime Achievement Award from the National Academy of Recording Arts and Sciences. A stroke brought his career to an end in April 1996, and he died in September just short of his 85th birthday.

Bill Monroe was able to bring off another first late in his career, one that involved a tiny gramophone. What was it?

His 1988 album, *Southern Flavor,* received the first bluegrass Grammy award.

Hank Williams inaugurated the golden age of country music.

CHAPTER FIVE

Hank, Lefty, and the Golden Age

For many, the 1950s are the *sine qua non* of country music. It's the era in which big stars, dressed in sequin-spangled cowboy suits, sang through their noses into oversized microphones at the Ryman Auditorium, crooning drinking and cheating songs to the whine of the steel guitar. As rural farm folks moved to the city to work in factories, the twang of country music reminded them of home; and from Baltimore to Bakersfield, they could hear it pouring from the jukebox of the neighborhood tavern.

The epicenter of the country star machine was Nashville, Tennessee, where the radio shows, record companies, and publishing houses that turned twang into capital had become a major commercial institution. Isolated from the pop music scene in California and New York, Nashville developed its own formulas for success, and the hits made on Music Row began to make an increasing impact on the pop charts. All that money and success would soon change country music forever; for a few golden years, though, it was honky-tonk heaven.

What is the enduring legacy to country music of the piano manufacturers, William Tonk and Brothers?

The upright grand piano they produced, with a decal that read "Ernest A. Tonk," may be the reason the taverns in which it was played came to be known as "honky tonks." That's one theory, anyway. The dictionary will tell you the origin of the term is unknown; but in the late 19th century, variety shows in the southwest, and the theatres that featured them, were referred to as "honkatonks." By the 1930s the term "honky tonk" was a standard name for roadhouse taverns in the southwest.

Many of those 1930s honky tonks shared a special kind of location. What was it?

They were often located just across the borderline of a county or state with dry laws that prohibited the sale of alcoholic beverages. This usually put them out in the middle of nowhere, which was also conducive to loud music and rowdy behavior.

What kind of music was first described as honky tonk?

It was a rough form of ragtime piano, heavy on the rhythm, that evolved into the style we call boogie-woogie. One of the first boogie-woogie piano hits was Meade "Lux" Lewis's "Honky Tonk Train Blues," which he first recorded in 1927.

What was the first application of the term "honky tonk" to country music?

East Texas singer Al Dexter's 1936 recording of a song called "Honky Tonk Blues."

What was the major stylistic contribution of honky tonks to the music that would bear their name?

Noise. Fill a little dive bar with a bunch of people drinking, dancing, engaging in loud conversation, and generally carrying on, and all of a sudden you can't hear the guitar and fiddle anymore. The changes in instrumentation associated with honky tonk, especially the move away from acoustic string instruments and the adoption of amplified electric guitars, microphones, and drums, was first and foremost an attempt by musicians to be heard over the roar of the audience. Of course, country singers and musicians soon discovered that the modern contraptions were capable of producing entirely new musical sounds, and they quickly adapted them to the down-home rhythms and harmonies they'd grown up with.

The honky-tonk clientele also contributed something that would have a major impact on the nature of honky-tonk songs. What was that?

 They had messed-up lives. The first honky tonkers were workers in the Texas and Oklahoma oil fields, ready to engage in a heavy drinking binge on payday, and then maybe a little gambling and a woman of easy morals. In short, honky-tonk music was the soundtrack to countless dysfunctional lives, and its themes centered around the preoccupations of working-class adults—including the pains of careless love, broken relationships, and life's other tragedies. No other genre has such a lock on whiskey and tears.

 All the elements of the tavern environment have been celebrated in country songs: swinging doors, neon lights, bar stools, and a particular piece of technology that would prove instrumental in the development of country music. Can you name this machine, which inspires lyrics of both joy and loathing?

 It's the jukebox, the coin-operated record player that became ubiquitous in bars and other places of amusement in the 1930s and 1940s. Jukeboxes were important to country in two ways: First, they allowed any little down-at-heels joint to have music, even if the establishment couldn't afford to hire a band. Second, the jukebox made the great country stars who arose in the 1930s and 1940s accessible to everyone, including those who couldn't buy records. The early *Billboard* magazine charts were little more than lists of the most popular songs on jukeboxes, so the machine, and the record distribution systems that were built around it, were integral to the Nashville star system.

Which came first, the jukebox or the juke joint?

Many people believe that the juke joint was named for the jukebox playing there, but it is the other way around. The term "juke joint" referred to drinking places favored by blacks in the Deep South, which were some of the early adopters of coin-op record machines. The term "juke" is of uncertain origin; some believe it is derived from the African-American Gullah dialect word "joog," meaning rowdy or disorderly. In any event, by the 1930s, the machine had taken its name from the establishment, in much the same way that honky-tonk music got its name.

Name one of the first big honky-tonk stars, a former share-cropper from Ryan, Oklahoma, who wrote the classics "I Love You So Much it Hurts" and "Slippin' Around."

It was Floyd Tillman, who turned from farming to music in 1934 and began playing with western swing bands. Tillman landed his first recording contract in 1940; he had a hit that year with his own composition, "It Makes No Difference Now." His jazzy style on both vocals and guitar brought a Jimmie Rodgers-like sophistication to country music. After serving in World War II, he began writing and recording some of the great honky-tonk standards; "I Love You So Much" and "Slippin' Around" were covered not only by virtually every honky-tonk singer, but by major pop stars of the day as well. While he decided to quit life on the road, he continued to write, penning more than 1,000 songs. Tillman died in 2003.

Finish the verse:
My sweetheart is gone, and I'm so lonesome
She said that she and I were through
So I started in drinking for pastime . . .

. . . Driving nails in my coffin over you.
Floyd Tillman recorded "Driving Nails in My Coffin" in 1946;
it later became a big hit for Ernest Tubb. The song is a perfect
expression of one of the central credos of honky-tonk songs:
When your baby leaves you, the appropriate response is to
head for a tavern and drink yourself to death.

Speaking of Mr. Tubb, where and when was Ernest Tubb born,
and how did he spend his formative years?

He was born in Crisp, Texas, in 1914, and grew up picking
cotton on his daddy's sharecropping stake. It was a pretty
typical existence for a poor farm boy, but Ernest had big
dreams; he loved the cowboy movies of Buck Jones and Tom
Mix, and became fascinated by the music of Jimmie Rodgers.
Ernest learned to yodel and pick guitar by imitating Rodgers's
records, and when his hero died in 1933, he moved to San
Antonio, where the Blue Yodeler spent his final days. He
managed to get a gig singing on the radio, while doing jobs
like driving a beer truck and digging ditches for the WPA.

In 1936, Ernest Tubb made a phone call that would change the course of his life. Who was on the other end of the line?

 Carrie Rodgers, Jimmie's widow. Ernest called her to introduce himself, and ask for an autographed photo of the Singing Brakeman. Carrie Rodgers listened to the young man sing on the radio and took a liking to him. She cleaned him up, bought him some decent clothes, and got him a recording contract with her husband's record company, RCA.

 Was his encounter with Carrie Rodgers a big break for Ernest Tubb?

 Not really. The records he made with RCA didn't go anywhere; despite the advice and promotional help of Rodgers's widow, Tubb was just one of many singers trying to cash in with a good Jimmie Rodgers impersonation in the wake of the Blue Yodeler's death. But Ernest saw Carrie Rodgers's support as a kind of anointing, and hit the road for good, honing his singing style in an endless series of little dive bars and radio stations between 1937 and 1940.

What 1939 event was largely responsible for Ernest Tubb's signature singing style?

He had his tonsils out. The effect of the surgery was to significantly lower his vocal register; Jimmie Rodgers's high, lilting yodel was now out of reach, and Tubb could no longer use the dead superstar as a crutch. Ernest Tubb began to write his own songs and develop his unique singing style.

While we're on the topic, what aspect of Ernest Tubb's voice is virtually unique among all the great stars of country music?

He couldn't really carry a tune. That would sink a singing career for most people, but Tubb used his meager vocal skills to develop an infectious style of sliding through notes, approximating those he couldn't hit. In his racy drinking and cheating songs, the slipping-and-sliding effect came across as charming and slightly inebriated; in heartfelt ballads, he could sound almost overcome with emotion. His style remains utterly original: While generations of country stars started off imitating Jimmie Rodgers or Hank Williams, no one ever quite imitated Ernest Tubb.

By 1940, Ernest Tubb had a new voice, a new delivery, and new, original songs. Was the package a hit?

Almost immediately. He recorded four sides for Decca records, and had his first successful single. One of his original numbers, "Blue Eyed Elaine," would be covered by Gene Autry. He also got a regular radio show on KGKO in Fort Worth.

In June 1940, Tubb's radio sponsor, Universal Mills, sent him on tour. What kind of venues did he play?

Grocery and feed stores. Tubb traveled from town to town throughout Texas promoting his sponsor's products as "The Gold Chain Troubadour."

What happened in 1941 that got Ernest Tubb off the feed-store circuit for good?

Decca released his all-time signature hit, "Walking the Floor Over You." On the strength of the record, he began appearing on the major barn dance radio shows, and was a regular member of the *Grand Ole Opry* by 1943.

In 1942, Ernest Tubb got to live a childhood dream. What was it?

He got to perform in two cowboy movies, *Fighting Buckaroo* and *Riding West,* for Columbia Pictures. Tubb would go on to be featured in several more films over the next five years.

What was the name of Ernest Tubb's band? And what bandleader gimmick did he pick up from Bob Wills?

His band, widely considered the best in country music, was The Texas Troubadours. Tubb adopted Bob Wills's habit of calling out the names of his musicians as they started in on an instrumental solo.

So when Tubb cried out "Aw, Billy" who was he introducing?

Electric guitar wizard Billy Byrd, who joined the Troubadours in 1949.

And who was the target of "Let's hear you, Bud!"

 Buddy Emmons, one of the early masters of the pedal steel guitar.

 How about "Here's Leon!"

 Leon Rhodes, who replaced Billy Byrd in 1960.

 Tubb's piano player in the 1950s went on to become legendary as a producer in the 1960s. Who was he?

Owen Bradley, a classically trained pianist who sometimes struggled with the low-down sound of honky tonk. As a record producer, Bradley was one of the architects of the pop-influenced Nashville Sound in the 1960s. We will return to him later.

In 1947, Ernest Tubb started a side business at 720 Commerce Street in Nashville. What line did he go into?

He opened the Ernest Tubb Record Shop, one of the first record stores dedicated to country music.

What radio program did Ernest start to promote his new store?

It was called the *Midnight Jamboree,* and it had a primo spot on WSM immediately following the *Grand Ole Opry* on Saturday nights. While the Opry focused on the big stars and old favorites, *Midnight Jamboree* audiences were treated to up-and-coming new artists, and Ernest Tubb used the program to help many young performers get their start in country music. The show made Tubb a Nashville institution; as WSM's second-longest running show, *Midnight Jamboree* celebrated its 60th anniversary in 2007.

Finish the verse:
As the warships left Manila
Sailing proudly o'er the seas
All the sailors' hearts were filled with fond regret
Looking backward to this island
Where they spent such happy hours . . .

. . . making love to every pretty girl they met.
"Filipino Baby," written by Billy Cox and Clarke Van Ness, was a hit for Ernest Tubb in 1946. It's the story of a Carolina boy who returns to the Philippines to marry the girl he fell in love with while stationed there in World War II.

Finish the verse:
The sun goes down
And leaves me sad and blue . . .

The iron curtain falls/on this cold war with you.
Floyd Tillman's song, "This Cold War with You," which turns mutual assured destruction into a romantic metaphor, was a hit for Tubb in 1949.

What do the Wilburn Brothers have in common with the Andrews Sisters?

They both did duet recordings with Ernest Tubb, as did many others, the most famous of which were his recordings with Red Foley in the early 50s and Loretta Lynn in the 1960s.

While we're playing six degrees of separation, what do Hank Williams, Hank Snow, Carl Smith, Patsy Cline, and Johnny Cash have in common, other than greatness, fame, and an enormous impact on country music?

They all got help early in their careers from Ernest Tubb, who got them radio appearances, took them on tour, offered professional guidance, and in general did all he could to help get them started.

Ernest Tubb helped another young singer-songwriter out by giving him a co-star spot on his syndicated television program in 1965. Who was this fellow Texan?

Billed each week as "the man who sings real pretty," it was none other than Willie Nelson, who had a much more buttoned-down look at the time than the outlaw image that would later make him famous.

Ernest Tubb has a cameo appearance in one of the biggest films of 1980. What was it?

Coal Miner's Daughter, the autobiographical film about Loretta Lynn. Sissy Spacek plays Loretta Lynn, and Ernest Tubb plays himself, introducing his protégé to a WSM radio audience.

Did the rise of the Nashville Sound in the 1960s eclipse Ernest Tubb's career, as it did with other honky-tonk artists?

 Not so's you could notice. Tubb went right on, appearing on the *Opry*, hosting the *Midnight Jamboree*, making hit records, and appearing in films and on television. His band hit the dance club circuit, playing hundreds of dates every year. It took emphysema to make him retire in 1982; he died in 1984 at age 70.

 He made his first record in 1946; seven years later, he was dead. But in that brief span he made an indelible mark, both on country music and on popular music in general. Name the boy from Mount Olive, Alabama, whom many consider the greatest country star of all time.

 Go on now—you know who we're talking about. Hiram Williams, known to history and legend as Hank, was born to Lon and Lillie Williams on September 17, 1923.

Did young Hank share the hard-scrabble existence of most rural folk during the 20s and 30s?

Hank grew up knowing what it was like to scratch for a living; his hard times were made even worse by two pieces of bad luck. He was born with a birth defect, spina bifida, that left him in near-constant pain. His father, a dirt farmer who went on to work in a lumber mill, had health problems of his own; a brain aneurysm sent him to a VA hospital for eight years, and Hank felt that he grew up without a father. Lillie Williams managed a boarding house in Georgiana, Alabama, and held a variety of odd jobs; Hank and his sister shined shoes and sold peanuts and newspapers to help make ends meet.

 In 1933, Hank was sent to live with his aunt and uncle in Fountain, Alabama. He only stayed a year, but he took away two things that would remain with him for the rest of his life. What were they?

 The guitar, which his Aunt Alice McNell taught him to play; and a love of whiskey, which his cousin J.C. introduced him to.

Who was Tee Tot?

That was the nickname of black street musician Rufus Payne, who befriended Williams on his return to Georgiana. The moniker referred to his habit of toting a mixture of tea and booze with him wherever he went. Payne became a mentor to Williams and taught him how to sing and play the blues.

How did Hank Williams get his first break in show business?

By the time his mother moved the family to Montgomery, Alabama, in 1937, Hank knew he wanted to make music for a living. The 14-year-old took to hanging around outside the Montgomery radio station WSFA, playing his guitar on the sidewalk. The station managers invited him in to play on the air; the audience response was so enthusiastic that Hank soon had his own 15-minute show on the station twice a week.

How was Hank billed on the show, and how much did he make?

Montgomery radio listeners knew him as "The Singing Kid," a gig that earned him a whole $15 a week.

What did Hank do with all that money?

 He used it to start his own band, which was soon playing clubs and parties all over central Alabama. By 1939, Hank dropped out of school so he could devote himself to his budding music career.

 What was the name of Hank's first band?

 He gave it the name he'd use for his backup musicians the rest of his career: "The Drifting Cowboys."

 Where did the Drifting Cowboys tour in 1941?

 Various military bases. They'd all been drafted, effectively breaking up the original band. Hank's spinal condition kept him out of the military, however, and he spent World War II working in the shipyards of Mobile. His attempts to keep his music career alive were often hampered by his propensity for showing up to gigs drunk.

In 1941, Hank got a chance to meet one of his heroes, Roy Acuff. Did the Nashville legend have any advice for Hank?

 Yep; he warned him to quit drinking. "You've got a million-dollar voice, son," Acuff is supposed to have told him, "but a ten-cent brain." The warning had little impact on Hank's drinking, and he was fired from his radio job in 1942.

 Hank's band began working with a female vocalist in 1943. Who was she?

 Audrey Mae Sheppard, whom he married a year later.

 Hank got his big break in 1946. What music industry giant gave it to him?

It was Fred Rose, who, along with Roy Acuff, had founded Acuff-Rose Publications, Nashville's most powerful music publisher. Rose first engaged Hank as a songwriter, but managed to get Williams his own MGM recording contract in 1947.

Hank's career got a further boost when he landed a regular spot on one of the biggest barn dance radio shows, one that rivaled the *Opry* in its reach and influence. What was it?

 The *Louisiana Hayride,* broadcast from the Municipal Auditorium in Shreveport over 50,000-watt KWKH. The powerful signal spread Hank's music all over the South. Hank Williams was the first of many country acts to get important early exposure on the *Hayride,* so much so that the show gained the nickname "Cradle of the Stars."

 For example, who was the young man who became a national sensation after his *Louisiana Hayride* appearances in the fall of 1954?

 Elvis Presley. The list of performers who got big breaks thanks to the *Hayride* reads like a list of country music royalty: Kitty Wells, Red Sovine, Webb Pierce, Faron Young, Jim Reeves, George Jones, and many, many more. The *Hayride* show continued in one form or another until the 1980s; at one point it was broadcast nationally by CBS.

 How did Hank's first records sell?

 He hit the charts immediately with two of his classic recordings, the doghouse anthem "Move it On Over," and the yodeling, two-step number, "Honky Tonkin'." He even had a hit with the old revival song, "I Saw the Light."

Identify the song:
She'll do me, she'll do you, she's got that kind of lovin'
Lord, I love to hear her when she calls me sweet baby...

That last word might be spelled "BAY-ee-ay-ee-ay-bee." It's from Hank's first #1 hit, "Lovesick Blues," his yodeling classic released in 1949.

Who wrote "Lovesick Blues?"

It wasn't Hank Williams. "Lovesick Blues" was a show tune written by Tin Pan Alley songwriters Cliff Friend and Irving Mills in 1922. It had been recorded several times previously, including a version by the blues great Bertha "Chippie" Hill.

Finish the verse:
You wore out a brand new trunk
Packing and unpacking your junk
Your daddy's mad, he done got peeved . . .

. . . Now you're gonna change, or I'm a-gonna leave.
Hank recorded "You're Gonna Change" in 1949.

According to Hank's song, "Lost Highway," what three things make up a drifter's life?

Just a deck of cards and a jug of wine/And a woman's lies makes a life like mine. "Lost Highway" was released as the B-side of "You're Gonna Change;" both sides hit the country charts in 1949.

His string of hits got Hank a new job in 1949. What was it? And were his new employers happy to have him?

He was invited to join the *Grand Ole Opry,* despite the producers' grave misgivings over his well-established reputation for drunkenness.

In 1950, Hank Williams recorded 14 sides under the name Luke the Drifter. Why the pseudonym?

To make sure the records didn't accidentally wind up on honky-tonk jukeboxes. Luke the Drifter sang the most sentimentally moralistic stuff—hardly what honky-tonk patrons wanted to hear. While there was never an attempt to pretend that Luke the Drifter wasn't Hank Williams, MGM was afraid that if jukebox distributors ordered the records, only to discover they weren't anything like "Honky Tonkin'" or "I'm So Lonesome I Could Cry," Williams's marketability would suffer; hence the name change.

Finish the verse:
The hogs took the cholera and they've all done died
The bees got mad and they left the hive
The weevils got the corn and the rain rotted the hay . . .

. . . But, we're still a-livin', so everything's okay.
"Everything's Okay" is one of Luke the Drifter's more upbeat numbers.

Were the Luke the Drifter numbers a hit?

Along with some gospel duets he recorded with Audrey, they were the only Hank Williams records released after 1949 that didn't make the country charts.

Pop superstar Tony Bennett had a 1951 hit with his rendition of "Cold, Cold Heart." What was the significance of that record?

It was the first recording of a Hank Williams song to go #1 on the pop charts. From that time on, pop producers recognized that there was gold in Hank's songs, and hits like "I Can't Help It (if I'm Still in Love with You)," "Hey, Good Lookin'," and "Half as Much" became chart-toppers for pop acts of the 1950s and beyond.

Something else happened in December of 1951 that wasn't much of a success for Hank. What was it?

 In an effort to ease the back pain that he felt fueled his drinking problem, he agreed to surgery. A long convalescence led to the breakup of his band. Alas, the operation had no effect on his pain, and Hank drank on.

 Almost as soon as he got out of the hospital, Audrey threw Hank out of the house. Who did he stay with?

 Up-and-coming country star Ray Price.

 What were the two main trends in Hank's career in 1952?

 His rise on the country record charts, and the disintegration of his performing career. Hank had five songs in the country top ten that year, all hitting either the #1 or #2 spots. They include classics like "Honky Tonk Blues," "Jambalaya," and "Half as Much." At the same time, he virtually gave up on live performing. His habitual drunkenness got him fired from the *Opry*, and he was reduced to occasional beer hall dates with pickup bands. He moved to Shreveport, where Fred Rose managed to get him back on the *Louisiana Hayride*.

Was his personal life as chaotic as his career?

Yes, and for the same reasons. Hank compounded his alcohol addiction by getting in trouble with morphine and other painkillers. The woman Hank was having an affair with became pregnant with his child, and he and Audrey divorced.

Did Hank Williams ever remarry?

Almost immediately. In October 1952, he married Billie Jean Jones Eshliman at the New Orleans Municipal Auditorium in a lavish ceremony before a paying crowd of 14,000.

How did Hank Williams spend New Year's Eve 1953?

He was stranded by a snowstorm at the Andrew Johnson Hotel in Knoxville, Tennessee, trying to get to a gig in Canton, Ohio, the next day. Bad weather kept him from flying, so he was forced to get to Ohio in his chauffer-driven Cadillac. He got a local doctor to shoot him up with a cocktail of B12 and morphine, and had to be carried to the back seat of the car. Early the next morning, his driver stopped for gasoline and discovered the singer already rigid; it is unknown how long the country superstar had been dead by then.

According to his death certificate, what killed Hank Williams?

Acute heart failure.

What was the name of the #1 country hit Hank Williams had in January, 1953, weeks after his death?

"I'll Never Get Out of This World Alive."

Which of the following Hank Williams classics were first released after his death: "Kaw-Liga," "Your Cheatin' Heart," or "I'm So Lonesome I Could Cry?"

If Hank was popular before his death, his untimely demise made him a hillbilly demigod. He had ten more charted hits between 1953 and 1989; even re-releases of his 1949 recording of "I'm So Lonesome" (in 1966) and "Why Don't You Love Me" (in 1976) were successful enough to make the charts. Hank's most popular song, "Your Cheatin' Heart," and the wooden Indian love song, "Kaw-Liga," were both debuted in 1953.

What was Hank Williams's last country hit?

In 1986, Hank Williams Jr. made a virtual duet with his father on a previously unreleased recording of "There's a Tear in My Beer." The song hit #7 on the country charts.

Is Hank Jr. his father's only child?

His only legitimate one; he fathered a daughter, Jett Williams, out of wedlock. She was born five days after his death.

He could croon the most syrupy ballad imaginable, and you could hear him harmonize on sacred songs with Hank Williams on the *Grand Ole Opry.* But he's best remembered for his novelty hits satirizing the deprivations of rural farm life. Who is this little-but-loud star that continues to appear on the *Opry* today?

Little Jimmy Dickens, the singer of such classics as "Take an Old Cold Tater (and Wait)," "Country Boy," and "A-Sleeping at the Foot of the Bed." Rural poverty may have been spiritually ennobling in other country songs, but Jimmy Dickens sang about growing up dressed in feed-sack clothes with nothing to eat but taters and corn bread, and about looking over an old gray mule each day. But he made you laugh—that and his crack *Opry* band made him a perennial favorite. He's a fixture at the *Opry* to this day, well into his 80s.

According to the imaginative curse that makes up the chorus of Little Jimmie Dickens's 1965 hit, "May the Bird of Paradise Fly Up Your Nose," what should happen to your wife?

May your wife be plagued with runners in her hose.

Who were the two hottest honky-tonk singers in the immediate wake of Hank Williams's death?

The unparalleled genius of Hank Williams often overshadows the careers of two performers who came on the scene at about the same time and were legends in their own right: Lefty Frizzell, whose iconic hits include "If You've Got the Money I've Got the Time" and "Always Late;" and Webb Pierce, famous for "There Stands the Glass" and "Why, Baby, Why."

What's Lefty Frizzell's real name? And how did he come by his nickname?

He was born William Orville Frizzell in Corsicana, Texas in 1928; high school buddies started calling him "Lefty" after he impressed them by punching out a fellow student with his left hand.

When did Lefty decide to become a country singer?

When he fell in love with the music of Jimmie Rodgers at age 12. He was soon singing in school programs, and was performing on the radio while he was still a teenager.

Lefty Frizzell wrote his classic song, "I Love You a Thousand Ways," in 1947. Where was he, and why?

In the county jail in Roswell, New Mexico, where he was doing six months for statutory rape. Three years later, the song would be his second #1 hit.

In "I Love You a Thousand Ways," Lefty sings, "Darlin' please wait, please wait until I'm free." Who was he pleading with?

His wife, Alice.

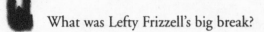

Q What was Lefty Frizzell's big break?

A He went to Dallas in 1950, hoping to impress legendary recording engineer Jim Beck. Beck made demo recordings of several of Lefty's songs, which he thought might be right for Little Jimmy Dickens. He played the demo of "If You've Got the Money" for Columbia Records producer Don Law, who signed Lefty immediately. Frizzell's first two records were #1 hits and he was on his way to making country music history.

Q Besides Lefty's rich, vowel-bending vocal, what's the most famous thing about his 1951 hit "Always Late (with Your Kisses)?"

A The steel guitar sting, a three-string run up the neck that's featured in the introduction and that punctuates the verses. Curly Walker's steel work was so popular that even today steel guitar players will throw the unique lead sting from "Always Late" into a solo to demonstrate that they're hip to Lefty Frizzell.

Q Besides recording #1 country hits, what else did Lefty have in common with Hank Williams?

A He drank heavily, and booze contributed to a number of stupid decisions. One of them was to fool around with an underage girl while on tour with Hank Williams in April 1951, a dalliance that led to his arrest for contributing to the delinquency of a minor.

Where was Lefty arrested?

In August 1951, he was arrested backstage at the *Grand Ole Opry*, where he'd become a member only a month before.

Despite his personal problems, Lefty Frizzell accomplished something in 1951 that would not be surpassed until 1964. What was this achievement, and who eventually broke his record?

Lefty Frizzell was the first recording act to have four *Billboard* top-ten hits at the same time. Not even Hank Williams ever surpassed that feat; the only artists to do so were the Beatles, who had five songs in the pop top ten simultaneously in 1964.

Lefty had another first in 1955. Name it.

He starred in the first country music show ever to play the Hollywood Bowl amphitheater.

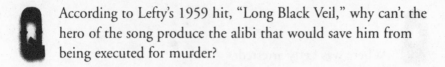

Q According to Lefty's 1959 hit, "Long Black Veil," why can't the hero of the song produce the alibi that would save him from being executed for murder?

A He had been in the arms of his best friend's wife. In an above-the-call display of discretion, our hero keeps silent about the tryst, as does she, which leads to his hanging and her hanging around his grave in the apparel that gives the song its name.

Q Finish the verse:
Now he's up there in Alaska
Diggin' in the cold, cold ground
The crazy fool is lookin'
For the gold I never found
It serves him right, and no one here is missin' him . . .

A *. . . Least of all the newlyweds of Saginaw, Michigan.*
Besides being a #1 hit for Lefty Frizzell in 1964, "Saginaw, Michigan" has the distinction of featuring more rhymes for "Michigan" than any other country song. It was also nominated for a Grammy.

Q In his 1974 hit of the same name, Lefty sings, "I never go around mirrors." Why not?

A "I can't stand to see a grown man cry." Lefty wrote the song with Whitey Schafer, who also collaborated with him on "That's the Way Love Goes."

With two new albums released by ABC Records in 1973 and 1974, Frizzell's career appeared poised for a resurgence. What prevented one from happening?

He was felled by a stroke in 1975. Thanks to Lefty's influence on stars like Merle Haggard and Willie Nelson, however, he is now often mentioned in the same breath as Hank as one of the two country giants who can be identified with one name.

Webb Pierce was another little boy who grew up with a serious Jimmie Rodgers addiction. Where was he born?

In West Monroe, Louisiana, in 1921. And Webb was his real name.

After he got out of the army in 1944, Webb Pierce moved to Shreveport, and tried for six years to break into the music business. What was his day job? And where did his first success come from?

He had a minor job singing on an early morning radio show, but he made his living selling men's furnishings at the local Sears Roebuck store. He finally got his break in 1950, when he was invited to appear on the *Louisiana Hayride* show.

Identify the song:
I pray ev'ry night
To the good Lord above
To send back to me
The one I really love...

"It's Wondering," Webb's first record. It went to the top of
the country charts in 1952, the first of three #1 records Webb
Pierce released in his debut year.

Finish the verse:
There stands the glass
Fill it up to the brim
Till my troubles grow dim . . .

. . . It's my first one today.
"There Stands the Glass" was another #1 hit for Webb Pierce,
despite the fact that some radio stations refused to play this
paean to self-medication.

Along with three #1 hits, what other distinction came Webb's
way in 1952?

He became a member of the *Grand Ole Opry*, on which he
would perform for the next four years.

In all, how many #1 hits did Webb Pierce have between 1952 and 1960?

He averaged almost two a year; he had a total of 14 chart-toppers and another 26 songs that hit the top ten. In 1959, "I Ain't Never" became a crossover hit on the pop charts.

 As the 1950s wore on, rock 'n' roll gradually began to push other kinds of pop music off the radio. How did Webb Pierce adapt?

By rockin', brother. In numbers like "Honky Tonk Song," "I Ain't Never," and "Teenage Boogie," the rhythm section takes over with a beat clearly intended to appeal to the teen audience. Today, many rockabilly fans consider Webb Pierce to be one of the fathers of the genre.

 Besides a string of classic country recordings, what is Webb Pierce best remembered for?

He was one of country music's first kings of bling. Between his successful recording career and lucrative business invest-ments, Webb had plenty of money, and he made damned sure everyone knew it. Nudie suits bedecked with rhinestones, a Cadillac studded with silver dollars, and a guitar-shaped swimming pool were a few examples of Webb's conspicuous consumption.

How did Webb Pierce's career fare after 1960?

His songs continued to visit the top ten until 1967, but he had no more #1 hits and by the late 1960s his star was in decline.

Webb Pierce recorded two duets in the mid-70s with an unlikely female star. Who was she?

Oddly enough, it was Broadway musical actress Carol Channing.

Webb did a more successful duet in 1982 on a remake of one of his classic hits. Who did he sing with, and what was the song?

He teamed up with Willie Nelson to record "In the Jailhouse Now," his last record to chart.

Is Webb Pierce still alive?

He died of pancreatic cancer in 1991; he was 69 years old.

It's a story we've told before: A young boy falls in love with Jimmie Rodgers records, gets a mail-order guitar and teaches himself to yodel. Only this little boy was born in Brooklyn, Nova Scotia. What was his name?

 He was born Clarence Eugene Snow in 1914, but you know him as Hank Snow, who, when he finally managed to break into the American market, became one of the biggest and longest-lasting stars of the honky-tonk era.

 Finish the verse:
I tried to warn you from time to time
But you just wouldn't listen, or pay me no mind . . .

 . . . So I'm movin' on.
"I'm Movin' On" was Hank Snow's breakthrough American hit in 1950.

 Did Hank Snow have a tough childhood?

 And how. His parents divorced when he was eight; he was sent to live with his grandparents, but kept running away to return to his mother. She married again, this time to a man who beat Hank repeatedly. In order to escape, Hank ran away to work on a fishing boat while still a young teenager. He soon caught the music bug, however, and at the age of 16 began playing clubs and bars in Halifax.

How did things go for young Hank in Halifax?

That's where his career took off. He married a singer, Minnie Blanch Alders, and the two formed a duet act. Before long they were singing on the radio.

As Hank's radio career got off the ground, he started billing himself with a Jimmie Rodgers-inspired handle. What was it?

Hank Snow was known as "The Yodeling Ranger." In 1936, he landed a record contract with RCA's Canadian Bluebird label, and a weekly radio show on the CBC network took his music from Montreal to the Yukon. Until 1949, he was Canada's biggest country star, and released 90 records, yet remained virtually unknown in the United States.

Hank did more than just sing. What was his other show business pursuit?

He toured with his horse, Pawnee, in a trick riding show.

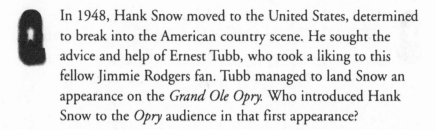 In 1948, Hank Snow moved to the United States, determined to break into the American country scene. He sought the advice and help of Ernest Tubb, who took a liking to this fellow Jimmie Rodgers fan. Tubb managed to land Snow an appearance on the *Grand Ole Opry.* Who introduced Hank Snow to the *Opry* audience in that first appearance?

Hank Williams. Hank Snow couldn't ask for better connections, but it took him two years to get his first breakthrough American hit record.

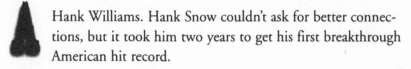 According to Hank Snow's signature hit, what is the significance of that lonesome whistle going down the track?

It means your true lovin' daddy ain't comin' back. "I'm Movin' On" spent 44 weeks on the country charts, topping out at #1. After a long wait, Hank Snow was an immediate star.

How many top-ten hits did Hank Snow have from 1950 through the mid-1970s?

43, including seven that went all the way to #1.

Hank's other signature hit is the rambling song, "I've Been Everywhere," in which a hitchhiker lists his travel destinations at an auctioneer's pace. Which of the following locations is not mentioned in the song?

a) Idaho
b) Tupelo
c) Jellico
d) Chicago

You're a good listener if you recognized that Tupelo is not one of the 92 destinations mentioned.

You can still hear one of Hank Snow's hits sung every Saturday night by the MC of one of radio's most popular shows. Which song? And who sings it?

Garrison Keillor, host of the long-running public radio variety show, *A Prairie Home Companion,* opens the show each week by crooning Hank's hit, "Hello Love."

By the 1970s, the pop influence had changed country music for good, and many former honky tonkers were singing pop- and rock-influenced material. Did Hank Snow follow suit?

Hank stuck to his honky-tonk sound, toured around the world, and even managed one last #1 hit, "Hello Love," in 1974, at age 59. He kept right on performing into his 70s, and died in 1999 at age 85.

Name the honky-tonk hitmaker whose classic recordings include "Don't Just Stand There," "Let Old Mother Nature Have Her Way," and "Hey Joe!"

Of course we're talking about Carl Smith, whose recording career lasted from 1951 until 1973. He was a member of the *Grand Ole Opry* in the early 50s and toured around the country later in the decade with the Phillip Morris County Music Show.

What did Carl Smith and Johnny Cash have in common?

A wife. Before she married Johnny Cash, June Carter was married to Carl Smith from 1952 to 1956.

She was born Muriel Ellen Deason in Nashville in 1919. During the Depression, she had to drop out of high school and work in a shirt factory to help her family make ends meet. But she would go on to become one of country music's greatest female stars. By what name do we remember her?

Muriel grew up in a musical family, and she married a singer, Johnnie Wright. When he teamed up with Jack Anglin to form Johnnie & Jack, Muriel did vocals for them; her husband started to bill her as Kitty Wells, a name from an old country song.

Johnnie & Jack managed to make it onto the *Louisiana Hayride*. Kitty also had a side job at KWKH; what was it?

She was a DJ, billed as the "Rag Doll."

Was Kitty Wells an avid performer?

She was really more of a homebody, the typical housewife of the era who cared more about tending to her kids than being a star. When some songs that she recorded in 1949 (in association with Johnnie & Jack's RCA record contract) failed to gain any traction, she almost left the music business for good. One of Johnnie & Jack's numbers, "Poison Love," did become a hit and gained the act a spot on the *Grand Ole Opry*.

In the opening of Kitty Wells's greatest hit, she sings, *As I sit here tonight, the jukebox playing/That tune about the wild side of life* . . . . The first two lines of the chorus go, *It wasn't God who made honky-tonk angels/As you said in the words of your song.* What song is she referring to?

"It Wasn't God Who Made Honky Tonk Angels" was written as a response to Hank Thompson's 1952 hit, "The Wild Side of Life." Here's the chorus of that song:
I didn't know God made honky tonk angels
I might have known you'd never make a wife
You gave up the only one who ever loved you
And went back to the wild side of life.

Was Kitty Wells excited about the chance to record "It Wasn't God Who Made Honky Tonk Angels?"

Not at all. For one thing, she was not burning with ambition to be in the music business to begin with. Besides that, a song that expressed the viewpoint of a fallen woman in a bar was sure to cause scandal in 1952; it was fine for the boys to sing about drinking and cheating, but for women, not so much, especially a woman with Kitty's gingham-and-lace image. Paul Cohen at Decca Records, to whom her husband had sent a demo tape, thought Kitty would be perfect for the song, and persuaded her to record it.

What two things greeted the release of "It Wasn't God Who Made Honky Tonk Angels?"

Success and scandal. The song rocketed to the top of the country charts, making Kitty Wells the first female artist to have a #1 country song. But fears about a puritanical reaction to the song proved well founded; the NBC radio network banned it, and the *Opry* refused to allow the song to be performed on the show.

How long did the song remain atop the country charts?

Six weeks. Only two country singers have ever topped that achievement (and they were both women).

Kitty Wells followed up her smash hit with another reply song written from the wronged woman's point of view. Can you name it?

Kitty replied to Webb Pierce's 1953 hit, "Back Street Affair," with her recording of "I'm Paying for That Back Street Affair," which also hit the top ten in 1953.

Finish the verse:
I have found a new love dear
And I'll always want him near
His lips are warm while yours are cold . . .

. . . Release me, darling let me go.
"Release Me" was a top-ten hit for Kitty in 1954.

Kitty's next #1 record was a duet. Who did she sing with, and what is the significance of that record?

In 1954, she recorded "One by One" with Red Foley. At the time, Kitty was the only solo female country star; but others would soon follow, and the practice of pairing male and female stars to make duet recordings became a country music mainstay (think George and Tammy, Porter and Dolly, Conway and Loretta, etc.).

Did success spoil Kitty Wells?

Never. Kitty didn't go in for the flashy clothes, cars, and lifestyle of a music superstar, preferring to maintain an image of purity and domestic bliss. On stage her dress was prim and proper, even a little old fashioned; at home she avoided scandal, and was once even photographed vacuuming the living room while husband Johnny Wright looked on. When their three children became old enough, they put together a family show that continued to tour until the 1990s. Her life was in sharp contrast with the tawdry scenes and emotional trauma she sang about, and that helped make her acceptable to audiences who could have strong feelings about a wayward woman.

Kitty Wells's last top-ten hit was 1965's "Meanwhile, Down at Joe's." How many top-ten singles did she release between 1952 and 1965?

Kitty didn't have many chart toppers, but she was a frequent entrant in the top-ten lists. In all, she had a total of 31 top-ten records, and her recordings continued to chart until 1979.

In 1974, Kitty recorded the album *Forever Young*. Her backing musicians were members of another popular music group. Can you name them?

Along with traditional country songs, the 55-year-old singer tried some blues and R&B numbers on the album, backed by members of the Allman Brothers Band. Although the album wasn't a commercial success, it did put Kitty Wells on the front lines of the revival of classic country sounds among the '70s rock generation—about which, more later.

In 1989, Kitty Wells was nominated for a Grammy. For which recording was she so honored?

She joined Brenda Lee, Loretta Lynn, and k.d. lang on the Honky Tonk Girls Medley that appears on lang's *Shadowland* album.

Kitty was back at the Grammys again in 1991 to accept a Lifetime Achievement Award. What three other musicians received the award that year?

Bob Dylan, John Lennon, and Marian Anderson. Kitty was only the third country singer ever to receive the award, and, as always, the first female country star.

His first hits were rockabilly numbers recorded for Sun Records, the label that had launched Elvis Presley's recording career. By 1956, he was recording numbers in a country vein, including two classic numbers he'd written while he was stationed in Germany with the air force. Who was this baritone from Kingsland, Arkansas?

 "Hello. I'm Johnny Cash." Growing up in the Arkansas cotton fields, Cash listened to gospel and country music on the radio; he was writing and performing gospel numbers himself while he was still in high school. After his air force stint, he married and moved to Memphis. While working a day job selling appliances, Cash would get together with his pals Luther Perkins and Marshall Grant to sing gospel on the radio. The group auditioned for Sam Phillips at Sun in 1954; he initially rejected their sacred songs, telling Cash to go home and come up with something Phillips could sell. He did just that—and his first rockabilly hits, "Cry! Cry! Cry!" and "Hey Porter," hit the charts in 1955.

 What were the two hits Cash wrote while in the air force?

 While in Germany, he wrote "Hey Porter," and his signature song, "Folsom Prison Blues," which became his first country top-ten hit in 1956.

According to the title of Johnny Cash's first #1 hit, what are you supposed to do when you get the blues?

 Get Rhythm. Cash followed up the song about the rockin' shoeshine boy with another #1 country single in 1956, "I Walk the Line," which also broke into the pop top twenty.

 How many #1 hits did Johnny Cash have over the next two decades, and how many made it to the pop top ten?

 Cash topped the country charts 14 times between 1956 and 1976, with classics like "Ring of Fire," "Ballad of a Teenage Queen," "Don't Take Your Guns to Town," "Sunday Morning Coming Down," and many more. His 1969 novelty hit, "A Boy Named Sue," was Cash's only entry on the pop top ten, and his only single to go Gold.

 Cash may have had only one Gold single, but two of his albums have gone Triple Platinum. They both had similar recording venues. What do the two albums have in common?

 They were both recorded live before audiences of incarcerated men. *At Folsom Prison* was released in 1968, followed by *At San Quentin* the next year. The raucous, wildly appreciative prison audiences seemed to bring out the best in Cash, and the albums produced two hit singles.

The way the story is told in the 2005 biopic, *Walk the Line,* his affair with June Carter saved Johnny Cash from a debilitating addiction to pills. True or false?

Mostly true. Cash had been touring with the Carter Sisters since the early 1960s; June Carter wrote Cash's hit "Ring of Fire," and their 1967 hit duet, "Jackson," won a Grammy. Maybelle's daughter loved Cash but she disapproved of his dissipated lifestyle. After the breakup of Cash's first marriage in 1966, June told him that she would only marry him if he cleaned up. But it took a month-long intervention by several Carter family members to finally get him off the pills. It worked, and Johnny Cash married June Carter in February 1968.

His top-ten hits include "Satisfied Mind," "Misery Loves Company," and "Green, Green Grass of Home." In his later years, he was the patriarch of the *Grand Ole Opry.* He's best remembered, however, for his long-running television show, on which he introduced one of the biggest female country stars. Who is the Missouri native with the blonde pompadour and the flashy Nudie suits?

Porter Wayne Wagoner, who was born in West Plains, Missouri, in 1927. He started singing on the radio in 1950, and after a few hard years on the road, had his first hits for RCA in the mid-50s. By 1957 he was a member of the *Opry.* But the turning point in Porter Wagoner's career came when the Chattanooga Medicine Company asked him to host a syndicated television show in 1960. The *Porter Wagoner Show* ran for 21 years, and Wagoner used it as a vehicle to present big stars and to introduce new talent like Willie Nelson and Waylon Jennings. His biggest find, however, came when he had to replace his female singer, Norma Jean, in 1967. He auditioned many singers, and finally selected Dolly Parton.

Were Porter and Dolly ever an "item"?

That's one of the great mysteries of country music. Both claimed that the relationship, while friendly, was purely professional. Parton left the *Porter Wagoner Show* in 1974 and ended her partnership with Wagoner, citing creative differences. But it's hard not to hear something deeper in Dolly's #1 hit, "I Will Always Love You," a break-up anthem she released shortly after her split with Porter. Dolly Parton became one of the dominant country and crossover stars of the 1980s, while Porter Wagoner's recording career went into decline. He continued to be a fixture on the *Opry*, though, and even released a critically praised album, *Wagonmaster*, in 2007, at the age of 80, a few months before his death from lung cancer.

His music could be heard in jukeboxes everywhere in the 1950s, from bobby-socks soda joints to the toughest honky tonks. We remember him best, however, for his great cowboy ballads. Who is this Arizona native?

 Little Jimmy Dickens discovered Marty Robbins doing a local television show in Phoenix in 1951. He was so impressed that he talked Columbia into giving Robbins a record contract and the *Opry* into giving him an appearance. Marty Robbins's first hits were rockabilly numbers, and teenagers were dancing to the pop-flavored "A White Sportcoat (and a Pink Carnation)" in 1957. He also had some honkin' hits with songs like "Singin' the Blues" and "Ruby Ann." But Marty Robbins will always be remembered for his western hit, "El Paso," and the smash album *Gunfighter Ballads and Trail Songs.* His recording career continued into the 1980s, including his Grammy-winning 1970 hit, "My Woman, My Woman, My Wife." Marty Robbins died of complications from heart surgery in 1982.

 From 1965 on, Marty Robbins always appeared in the last segment of the *Grand Ole Opry.* Why?

 So he could drive a racecar at the Nashville Speedway on Saturday nights. When a show ran late one night in 1968 and he was in danger of losing stage time, he simply kept playing past the show's scheduled end. Marty Robbins made a tradition of it, sometimes extending the *Opry* broadcast by an hour or more.

Who sang this hit?
I'm a honky-tonk man
And I can't seem to stop
I love to give the girls a whirl
To the rhythm of an old jukebox
But when my money's all gone
I'm on the telephone
Hollerin' "Hey, hey mama, can your daddy come home?"

It was Johnny Horton, whose first hit was "Honky Tonk Man" in 1955. He later became known for his "saga songs," including smash hits like "The Battle of New Orleans" and "North to Alaska."

Name the honky tonker born in Shreveport, Louisiana whose hits include "If You Ain't Lovin'," "Hello Walls," and "Live Fast, Love Hard, Die Young."

It's Faron Young, whose honkin' hits were on every country jukebox between 1954 and 1962. A protégé of Webb Pierce, Young flirted with the Nashville Sound in the early 60s before returning to hard country with 1969's "Wine Me Up," and "It's Four in the Morning" in 1971. His recording career petered out in the 1980s, and he committed suicide in 1996.

Although a variety of rhythms were featured in country songs, most were either in 4/4 time with an emphasis on the first and third beats (like Hank Williams's "Your Cheatin' Heart") or in 3/4 waltz time (like Ernest Tubb's "Waltz Across Texas"). Beginning in 1956, however, a new rhythm would take over country jukeboxes, one that would come to define the honky-tonk sound. What was the rhythm, and who was the innovator who would lend the beat his name?

The shuffle, a 4/4 time on which each beat is equally stressed, creating a bouncy, infectious rhythm that's tailor-made for dancing. It burst on the scene in Ray Price's first smash hit, "Crazy Arms," which spent 20 weeks at #1 in 1956. Price developed his style even further throughout the late 50s in songs like "Heartaches by the Number" and "City Lights." The dance rhythm was picked up by many other honky-tonk acts and became known as the "Ray Price Beat."

Hailing from Perryville, Texas, Ray Price's country music career was flying below the radar before he was introduced to another musician in 1951. Who was it?

A good friend to have—Hank Williams. Hank took a liking to Ray, took him on tour with him, and wrote him a song to record, "Weary Blues," that charted well enough to get Price a spot on the *Grand Ole Opry* in 1952. As we discussed earlier, when Hank's wife threw him out of the house, he roomed with Ray, which is where he met his second wife.

Along with his shuffle beat, Ray Price was known for his hot band. What was their name?

The Cherokee Cowboys.

What do Rodger Miller, Willie Nelson, and Johnny Paycheck have in common?

They were all, at one time or another, members of the Cherokee Cowboys.

Besides its shuffle beat, "Crazy Arms" features another innovation, one that involves a fiddle style. What was it, and who is the ubiquitous Nashville session pro who plays it?

It's the great Tommy Jackson, who moved away from the countrified double-stop figures most Nashville fiddlers relied on and developed a sinuous single-string style that contributed to the record's sophisticated, uptown sound. Tommy Jackson went on to become the hottest session fiddler in town; that's him you hear on nearly all of Ray Price's big hits, along with hundreds of other country chart toppers recorded in the 50s and 60s.

Finish the verse:
You took the laughter from this world of mine
And thanks to you the sun will never shine
Walked the floor so much, wore out my shoes . . .

. . . Received your invitation to the blues.
"Invitation to the Blues," written by Rodger Miller,
was a 1958 hit for Ray Price.

Patsy Cline on the stage of the *Grand Ole Opry*.
Considered one of the greatest country singers of all,
her crossover success hastened the decline of classic country sounds.

CHAPTER SIX

From Nashville to Bakersfield:

The End of Classic Country, and Beyond

The crossover bonanza that country music enjoyed in the 1950s was in steep decline by the end of the decade, as rock 'n' roll claimed the enthusiastic loyalty of the Baby Boom generation. With their copious streams of cash flow slowing to a trickle, record producers were desperate to revive their fortunes. Country music had always flirted with songs and sounds from pop; as the 1960s dawned, however, Nashville's top session producers went after pop audiences with a vengeance, abandoning the twang of fiddles and nasal vocals for the lush sounds of strings and background vocal quartets. What they created came to be known as the Nashville Sound, and it accomplished its mission, generating monster crossover hits. But the formula of blending country with pop and rock to appeal to a wider audience became so widely established that, by the 1970s, it became difficult to tell which genre was which. There are those who will argue that the Nashville Sound killed "real" country music for good.

But the reaction to the pop-oriented Nashville Sound was immediate. Whether because of class and regional allegiances, or because of a spiritual identification with country themes and attitudes amid America's industrial urban wasteland, the demand for classic country lived on. On the West Coast, a new country mecca rose, one that prospered with a harder-edged sound. And if country was absorbing rock, rock was falling in love with the fiddle and steel guitar, introducing classic country sounds to the enormous youth market of the 1970s. As the century drew to a close, various renegades had dedicated themselves to reviving and re-establishing "authentic" country music, and their efforts gained them a large and loyal audience. As the alt country movement demonstrates today, classic country ain't dead yet—not by a long shot.

The first appearance of the "Nashville Sound" in a major publication was in a 1960 *Time* feature story, in which the phrase appears in a subhead. Which country star, whose music helped define the Nashville Sound, did the story profile?

Jim Reeves, of Panola County, Texas, whose hits included "Four Walls," "He'll Have to Go," "Blue Side of Lonesome," and many more. Reeves was another Jimmie Rodgers fan as a youngster, but he was also influenced by the pop crooning of Bing Crosby and Frank Sinatra, and set Eddie Arnold as his model for country success.

What career path did Jim Reeves share with Roy Acuff?

Before he was a country singer, he was a baseball player. Reeves won a baseball scholarship to the University of Texas, and after a stint as a welder during World War II, played several seasons of minor league ball in the St. Louis Cardinals' farm team system. In 1947, a leg injury ended his baseball career, and he went to work as a radio announcer and DJ in East Texas and Louisiana.

What was Jim Reeves's big musical break?

While he was working as an announcer on KWKH radio in Shreveport, one of the acts scheduled to appear on the *Louisiana Hayride* failed to show, and Reeves was asked to fill in. He was a hit, and was soon recording for small Texas labels.

Finish the verse:
He makes the night spots all along the bay,
People want to see him when he comes their way,
He spreads so much joy everywhere he goes . . .

. . . Everyone shouts "Viva la Mexican Joe."
"Mexican Joe" was Jim Reeves's first #1 country hit in 1953, the first of a string of novelty numbers he recorded for Abbot Records. While they did well enough on the country charts to gain him a spot on the *Grand Ole Opry* in 1955, Jim Reeves had yet to find the rich, intimate style that would make him a superstar.

In 1955, Jim Reeves got out of his Abbot Records contract and signed with RCA. There, he began to work with a producer whose perfectionism and skill in blending country and pop idioms made him one of the chief architects of the Nashville Sound. Although he was tremendously influential behind the scenes, most folks remember him for his virtuoso guitar work. Who are we talking about?

Chet Atkins. Chester Burton Atkins learned to play guitar while a boy in Tennessee, and as a teenager he became entranced by Merle Travis's picking style. He soon eclipsed the master, and was in hot demand as a recording session guitarist and in the bands of acts that appeared on the *National Barn Dance* and the *Grand Ole Opry*. He had a solo instrumental hit with a countrified version of "Mister Sandman" in 1955. Spending all that time in the studio, Atkins picked up the skills of a producer, and was soon arranging and directing recording sessions himself. In 1955, RCA made Chet Atkins the head of its Nashville studio.

One of Chet Atkins's earliest experiments with a de-countrified sound occurred in 1957 with "Oh, Lonesome Me." With which singer-songwriter was he collaborating?

Don Gibson, who wrote "Oh, Lonesome Me," and such other classic country songs as "Sweet Dreams" and "I Can't Stop Loving You." It was while recording "Oh, Lonesome Me" that he and Atkins decided to dispense with the steel guitar and fiddle and add backup singers; the result was Gibson's first #1 hit record. Gibson had a string of hits through the 50s and 60s and wrote hundreds of songs that entered the country repertoire; "I Can't Stop Loving You" alone has been recorded more than 700 times.

Chet Atkins transformed Jim Reeves's sound, setting him intimately close to the microphone and supporting him with backup singers and a string section. The new style soon bore fruit. What slow crooning Jim Reeves number went to #3 on the country charts in 1957?

 "Am I Losing You?" was followed up later in 1957 by Reeves's #1 hit, "Four Walls."

 What two items of technology are mentioned in Jim Reeves's 1960 smash hit, "He'll Have to Go?"

 Oh, let's sing that first verse, shall we?
*Put your sweet lips a little closer to the **phone***
Let's pretend that we're together all alone
*I'll tell the man to turn the **jukebox** way down low*
And you can tell your friend there with you he'll have to go…

 What significant contribution to the evolution of country music belongs to "He'll Have to Go?"

 It was Jim Reeves's first record to succeed on both the country and pop charts, hitting #1 in country and #2 in pop. It was an international hit as well. It was the first—but by no means the last—time that blending country and pop would result in huge crossover success for the Nashville Sound. Soon, record labels were looking beyond their traditional fan base and attempting to duplicate Jim Reeves's success.

What do South African Zulus, Norwegian music fans, and Indian guru Meher Baba have in common?

They're all nuts about Jim Reeves. Reeves is beloved in South Africa as the star of one of the nation's most popular films, *Kimberley Jim,* which he filmed in 1963; among the Zulus, he's known as "King Jim." Reeves had 17 top-ten records in the Norwegian charts, including three #1 hits. And you can find Jim Reeves's music in any record store in India; "There's a Heartache Following Me" and "Welcome to My World" were particular favorites of Sri Baba, a guru with many western devotees.

Jim Reeves stopped recording for RCA in 1964. Why?

On July 31, after a trip to look at some property he was considering, he and his business manager climbed into a small airplane to head for home. Jim was piloting as the plane encountered a thunderstorm near Nashville; Reeves became disoriented, turned the plane upside down, and, in a mistaken attempt to get above the storm, barreled straight into the ground. His body was discovered two days later.

In the 1940s, he billed himself as the "Tennessee Plowboy" when he left Pee Wee King's band to start a solo career. He laid the foundation for the Nashville Sound in the late 40s with crossover hits like "Anytime" and "Bouquet of Roses." His career declined somewhat in the 50s, but in the wake of Jim Reeves's success he returned with a vengeance in the mid-1960s, releasing a string of hits that rode both the country and pop charts. Name him.

It's Eddy Arnold, the king of country crossover. Arnold's voice never did have the harder edge of other country stars, but was tailor-made for the kind of crooner ballads that made him famous. When Nashville went pop in the 60s, the lush arrangements of strings and backup singers fit his style perfectly in songs like "What's He Doing in My World," "Tip of My Fingers," and "Make the World Go Away," which hit both the country and pop top ten in 1965.

According to Eddy Arnold's 1968 hit, what can you do after you've told me you love me for a thousand years?

Then you can tell me goodbye—if it doesn't work out, that is. "Then You Can Tell Me Goodbye" was Eddy's last #1 hit—the last of 28 over his long career, one that covered records, radio, and television and lasted until the 1980s.

Eddy Arnold and Elvis Presley had something in common besides voices made in heaven. What was it?

Actually, the question should be who was he: their manager, Col. Tom Parker, who guided Eddy's career during his Tennessee Plowboy period.

Eddy Arnold: alive or dead?

After years of various health problems, Eddie Arnold died on May 8, 2008, at a care facility near Nashville. He was only a few days short of his 90th birthday.

One of the things that made the Nashville Sound so distinct is the fact that many of the same great musicians performed on hit after hit, called in by Music Row producers to provide backup for the latest star. For example, one of the signature Nashville Sound touches is that slinky piano, full of whole-note slurs. Name the pianist who created the sound, and who had his own hit instrumental version of "Last Date."

Floyd Cramer, who wrote "Last Date" at the insistence of Chet Atkins to exploit the "slip-note" style for which Cramer is famous. A self-taught musician, Cramer came to Nashville in the early 50s, playing the plinky honky-tonk piano style that had been made popular on the records of Lefty Frizzell. Thanks to a shortage of session pianists, the talented Cramer found plenty of work, and befriended Chet Atkins, who made him a cornerstone of the pop-influenced sound he was creating.

How about those rich, tight male vocal harmonies? Name the gospel quartet who provided them.

Founded by two young evangelists, the Jordonaires made a series of successful gospel records for Decca and Capitol in the early 50s before becoming a session backup group. Upon joining the RCA stable, they worked nearly constantly, and can be heard on the recordings of Eddy Arnold, Jim Reeves, Patsy Cline, Red Foley, and in general, everybody who was anybody.

In one year alone, the Jordonaires sang on recordings that sold a cumulative total of 33 million copies. What year was it? And who was the artist responsible for the biggest chunk of those sales?

It was 1957, the year the Jordonaires performed on all five of Elvis Presley's #1 hits.

If the Nashville Sound recording you're hearing features female backing vocals, who are you probably listening to?

The Anita Kerr Singers, who started out doing backup singing at Decca Records before becoming part of the RCA stable in 1961. Along with providing backups for records by Nashville stars like Jim Reeves and Patsy Cline, the Anita Kerr Singers can be heard on pop records by stars like Perry Como and Bobby Vinton as well.

Q And what would the Nashville Sound be without strings? The replacement of steel guitars with string sections is one of the principal elements that made the "countrypolitan" sound. Which musicians often provided those shimmering strings?

A They were often pickup ensembles drawn from members of the Nashville Symphony Orchestra.

Q He started out as a bandleader, but his interest in songwriting and arranging got him work as a record producer for Decca. In that capacity, he produced the recordings of such luminaries as Roy Acuff, Bill Monroe, and Ernest Tubb. It is his work you hear on Red Foley's million-selling "Chattanoogie Shoe Shine Boy" and Kitty Wells's smash hit, "It Wasn't God Who Made Honky Tonk Angels." Who was this son of Westmoreland, Tennessee?

A It was Owen Bradley, who became Nashville's first independent producer in 1955 when he built his own state-of-the-art home studio.

Bradley later expanded the house he recorded in with a metal structure that gave his studio its legendary nickname. What was the structure?

 It was an army-style Quonset hut. Two genres were brought to fruition at the Quonset Hut: rockabilly, which was born with Gene Vincent's "Be-Bob-a-Lula" in 1956; and the quintessence of the Nashville Sound, Owen Bradley's classic recordings of Patsy Cline. Brenda Lee and Loretta Lynn were also beneficiaries of Owen Bradley's genius for production.

 Let's talk about country's greatest female star, whose recordings both epitomized the Nashville Sound and contributed to the demise of classic country by beguiling country record producers with dreams of crossover success. What was Patsy Cline's birth name?

 She was born Virginia Patterson Hensley in Winchester, Virginia, in 1932. Virginia had a tough enough childhood; sexually abused and deserted by her father, she dropped out of school as a teenager to help support her family. Determined to become a star, she started singing in the local honky tonks.

Who was Virginia Hensley trying to imitate as she formed her vocal style?

There were few big female country stars to imitate in the mid-40s; Virginia's tastes leaned toward Kay Starr, Helen Morgan, Kate Smith, and other pop divas of the day. She was also a fan of Charlene Arthur, a regional favorite who had a low-down, bluesy style.

How did Patsy Cline get her stage name?

She made up the Patsy part out of her middle name; the last name she got by marrying Gerald Cline in 1953. The two split up a few years later, but she would keep his name on stage, even long after she remarried.

Fans of the 1985 movie biography of Patsy Cline, *Sweet Dreams,* will recall the early high point of the film in which she appears on *Ted Mack's Amateur Hour,* a TV talent show. Was that a big break for the young amateur?

In fact, Patsy Cline had been on TV for almost a year when she appeared on the *Ted Mack* show in July 1955. She had been featured on the *Town & Country* show, a regionally syndicated program featuring up-and-coming artists like Jimmy Dean and Roy Clark. Patsy had quite a following in the Washington D.C. music scene at the time, and she had even released four singles, none of which managed to chart. The *Ted Mack* appearance did help the song she performed on the show, "Walking After Midnight," become Patsy's first hit, and a big one; it made #2 on the country charts and almost broke into the pop top ten.

What was Patsy Cline's stage get-up like at this point in her career?

Patsy adopted the persona of a spunky cowgirl, singing bouncy numbers full of yodels and growls, and appearing in fancy western outfits, complete with hat and fringe.

Did having a big hit with "Walking After Midnight" make Patsy Cline a star?

It looked like it was going to at first; she rode the hit for months, and even managed to land more national television appearances. But she couldn't seem to generate a follow-up, and by 1957 she was looking like a one-hit wonder. She remarried, had a baby, and dropped out of the music scene for a time.

Another memorable moment in *Sweet Dreams* is when Patsy meets her new manager, Randy Hughes, who tells her if she concentrates on slow ballads, she'll be a big star. More cinematic fiction?

In part. Randy Hughes did help Patsy Cline revive her career, pushing her to tour extensively and eventually getting her a spot on the *Grand Ole Opry*. But the emphasis on slow, emotional ballads came from her producer, Owen Bradley, who used Patsy's voice to refine and perfect his countrypolitan sound. Interestingly enough, Owen Bradley doesn't appear as a character in *Sweet Dreams*.

According to the words of Patsy Cline's first #1 hit, what happens every time someone speaks your name?

 "I Fall to Pieces." Patsy had to be pressured into accepting Owen Bradley's arrangement, which was replete with string section and backing vocals by the Jordonaires. Along with topping the country charts, the record went to #12 on the pop charts, proving that Bradley's instincts were correct.

 As everyone familiar with the Patsy Cline legend knows, in 1961, just as "I Fall to Pieces" was climbing the charts, Patsy was involved in a head-on auto collision that threw her into the windshield, nearly killing her. Which friend of hers arrived on the scene and began to pick the glass from her face?

 Future country star Dotty West, one of a number of young female artists Patsy befriended and encouraged. The most famous, of course, is Loretta Lynn, but others included June Carter, Barbara Mandrell, and Brenda Lee. In a stroke of tragic irony, Dotty West was herself killed in an automobile accident in 1991.

How long did it take for Patsy Cline to recuperate from her accident?

Not long, considering that she had a badly dislocated hip along with a lacerated face. She spent a month in the hospital, but was determined to get back on the road to capitalize on the success of "I Fall to Pieces" and to promote the new single she was about to release. She was still on crutches when she started touring again, using wigs and makeup to hide the prominent scar on her forehead.

Patsy resumed touring just in time for the release of what we remember as her greatest hit, "Crazy." First the gimme question: Who wrote "Crazy?"

Willie Nelson, who released his demo recording years later on his *Crazy: The Demo Sessions* CD. The story goes that Willie, at the time an up-and-coming Nashville songwriter, was so nervous about Patsy's reception of the song that he waited outside in the car as she listened to the demo. His apprehension was justified; Patsy hated the song, felt she couldn't sing it, and got into a shouting match with Owen Bradley when he insisted. With a revised arrangement of the song, Patsy was convinced to give it a try, and the rest is county music history.

"Crazy" is one of the best-loved ballads in American popular music. Did it top both the pop and country charts?

Incredibly, it topped neither. It did all right, though, hitting #2 in both the country and pop listings. More importantly, the back-to-back success of "I Fall to Pieces" and "Crazy" established Patsy Cline as a bona fide star.

Finish the verse:
I've got the records that we used to share
And they still sound the same as when you were here
The only thing different, the only thing new . . .

. . . I've got the records, she's got you.
"She's Got You" was another crossover hit for Patsy Cline in 1962, topping the country charts and coming in at #3 in the pop charts.

As we all know, by the time "She's Got You" was released in January 1962, Patsy Cline had little more than a year to live. How many more top-ten hits did she have in that time?

Only two, and they both barely scraped the bottom of the country top ten. The rocking "When I Get Through With You" got no farther than #10 in 1962, and the last single she released in her lifetime, "Leavin' On Your Mind," topped out at #8 in early 1963.

Another plane crash, another music legend lost. While flying home from a benefit concert on March 5, 1963, the small plane she was in ran into high winds and crashed. Where did her plane come down? And who died in the crash with her?

The wreckage was found near Camden, Tennessee, only 90 miles from Patsy's Nashville home. She was accompanied by her manager, Randy Hughes, who was flying the plane, and by fellow *Grand Ole Opry* stars Cowboy Copas and Hawkshaw Hawkins.

Did Patsy's star burn even brighter upon her untimely demise?

Not judging by her record sales: "Sweet Dreams," one of her classic songs, released a few months after her death, was a #5 country hit but didn't make the pop top ten; "Faded Love," another signature hit released in 1963, only made #7 on the country charts and failed to make the pop charts at all. As the 60s moved on, the Nashville music scene left Patsy's country chanteuse sound behind, and none of her posthumously released singles after "Faded Love" made the country top ten during the decade.

Two decades after her death, a Patsy Cline revival occurred. Identify the two events that spurred it.

In 1982, a virtual duet paired Patsy Cline and Jim Reeves doing "Have You Ever Been Lonely;" the song hit #5 on the country charts. Then, of course, there was Jessica Lange's engaging portrayal of Patsy and her warfare of love with her second husband, Charlie Dick (played by Ed Harris), in the 1985 hit movie *Sweet Dreams.* By the time alt country singer k.d. lang released her first album in 1989, with its obvious stylistic homage to Patsy (her backup band was even named "the Reclines"), there was a new generation of Patsy Cline fans ready to receive it.

The Decca compilation, *Patsy Cline's Greatest Hits,* holds what distinction?

It is the only album by a country artist first recorded before 1960 to sell more than seven million copies. By contrast, 90s superstar Reba McEntire's best-selling album has only sold over four million copies.

Even the king of honky tonk went pop in the 1960s. Who had hits with "Danny Boy" in 1967 and "For the Good Times" in 1970?

It was Ray Price. Price's pop hits were big sellers, despite the disgruntlement of his honky-tonk fans to the string-laden arrangements. The Kris Kristofferson song, "For the Good Times," was a #1 country song and made the pop top 20 as well. But Price's five pop singles were to be his last chart topping hits; he struggled through the 80s and 90s, moving from label to label and never hitting on a formula that clicked.

He burst on the honky-tonk jukeboxes in the mid- to late 50s with classic compositions such as "Color of the Blues," "The Window Up Above," and "Tender Years." Nashville changed, but he never did, and he clung to his hard-country sound long enough to see it return to popularity. Name the performer many consider to be second only to Hank Williams as country's greatest singer-songwriter.

George Glenn Jones was born in a log cabin in Saratoga, Texas, in 1931, and learned to love music at the local Baptist church and the tavern outside of town. Growing up in a housing project with an abusive alcoholic for a father, George Jones found escape in the music of Roy Acuff, Hank Williams, and Lefty Frizzell. He started singing on the radio in the late 40s, but his first hit record didn't come until 1955.

According to the words of George Jones's first #1 hit, what's mighty, mighty pleasin'?

 Your pappy's corn squeezins. "White Lightning," a rockin' honky-tonk number about the travails of the moonshiner, brought George Jones to national attention in 1959.

 Besides an unforgettable voice and a way with a song, what did George Jones have in common with his hero, Hank Williams?

 A regrettable addiction to alcohol. Jones inherited both his daddy's alcoholism and his violent temper, and the two together ruined his first three marriages and almost ended his career. In the 1970s, his penchant for being too drunk to show up for work earned him the nickname "No Show Jones."

 Finish the verse:
Just because I ask a friend about her
Just because I spoke her name somewhere
Just because I rang her number by mistake today . . .

 . . . She thinks I still care.
George Jones had a #1 country hit with "She Thinks I Still Care" in 1962.

George Jones had a 1963 hit singing a duet with a female country star on "We Must Have Been Out of Our Minds." Who was she?

If you answered Tammy Wynette, you're a few years too early. Jones recorded "We Must Have Been Out of Our Minds" with Melba Montgomery, who had been the female singer with Roy Acuff's band before striking out on her own. The song hit #3 on the country charts, which prompted Jones and Montgomery to release four more duet singles, none of which were as successful.

What's the significance of George Jones's 1971 top-ten hit, "Take Me?"

It's his first single featuring a duet with his third wife, Tammy Wynette. Tammy grew up picking cotton and singing gospel songs in Itawamba County, Mississippi. She started singing on a local TV show while working at a beauty salon and being a single mom to three daughters (she divorced her first husband in 1965). By the time she married Jones in 1969, she'd been through another marriage and had released her classic country hits, "Your Good Girl's Gonna Go Bad," "I Don't Wanna Play House," "D-I-V-O-R-C-E," and, of course, "Stand By Your Man."

Relate the story of how George won Tammy.

According to the tale, in 1968 George witnessed a knock-down drag-out fight between Tammy and her second husband, singer-songwriter Don Chapel. Jones offered to take Tammy and her daughters away with him, and they climbed into his car and left Chapel behind. George and Tammy's marriage lasted until 1975 and produced a daughter and a string of legendary country duets.

George and Tammy issued 13 duet singles between 1971 and 1980. How many went to #1?

Just three: "We're Gonna Hold On" (1973), "Golden Ring" (1976), and "Near You" (1976). George and Tammy also released nine duet albums, including the 1976 chart topper *Together Again,* which appeared a year after their divorce.

There are many who will argue that George Jones's "He Stopped Loving Her Today" is the greatest country song every written. Few would disagree that the song is a classic old-school country weeper. When did Jones record it?

Not until 1980, when it hit #1, became his first million-selling single, and won him a Grammy for Best Male Country Vocal Performance. When you consider that the dominating country acts of the era included Anne Murray, Kenny Rogers, and a very pop-oriented Dolly Parton, it's remarkable that Jones had such success with a song that would have been right at home on a honky-tonk jukebox in 1960.

Where was "Nashville West"?

That's the name that many California country fans used to refer to Bakersfield, in Kern County. Situated in the heart of farm and oil territory in the southern San Joaquin Valley, it was a magnet for the Okies and Arkies who fled the Dust Bowl in the 1930s. They brought their musical tastes with them, and by the 1940s, Bakersfield was one of the hubs of country music. Because of its isolation from the main scene in Nashville, Bakersfield never felt the pressure to accommodate itself to the pop trends of the 50s and 60s, and the musicians there retained the harder-edged sound of the southwestern dance halls. As a result, by the mid-60s, the music coming out of the region became known as the Bakersfield Sound, and was treasured by fans who felt that Nashville had sold out to pander to pop audiences.

Name the son of Texas sharecroppers who would become king of the Bakersfield Sound.

Alvin Edgar Owens Jr., who everybody started calling Buck. Buck Owens's family headed west in 1937, settling in Arizona. Buck dreamed that music might take him away from the hard work and hard times he grew up with; by the time he was a teenager he was playing in the local honks, soaking up musical influences from western swing to tejano to rhythm & blues. He married Bonnie Owens in 1951, and the two put together a band that found a home in Bakersfield. Soon, Buck was a popular session guitarist in the recording studios of Hollywood, and began to build a following at the Blackboard, a Bakersfield dance club.

In 1956, California label Pep Records released a rockabilly single, "Hot Dog," by Corky Jones. Who was Corky Jones?

It was a pseudonym for Buck Owens, who didn't want country fans to think he was a rock 'n' roller. By 1957, Buck got a recording contract with Capitol Records; his first chart hit, "Second Fiddle," appeared in 1959.

Finish the verse:
I'll play the part about a man that's sad and lonely
And beggin' down upon his bended knee
I'll play the part, and I won't need rehearsin' . . .

. . . *'Cause all I gotta do is act naturally.*
"Act Naturally" was Buck Owens's first #1 hit in 1963,
the first of many as the popified Nashville Sound otherwise
dominated country music over the next six years.

Who recorded a popular cover version of "Act Naturally"
in 1965?

None other than the Beatles, whose straight country performance, with Ringo Starr doing a plaintive, off-key vocal, was
rock's first homage to the Bakersfield Sound. There would be
many more to come, as young audiences rediscovered country
music in the late 60s and early 70s and found the twang they
were looking for on Buck Owens records. Many years later,
Buck and Ringo recorded a duet version of "Act Naturally."

An ace guitarist himself, Buck Owens was known for his first-
rate band. What was their name?

The Buckaroos, including Don Rich, who played guitar and
sang those high, tight harmonies with Buck, Tom Brumley on
pedal steel, Willie Cantu on drums, and Doyle Holly on bass.
Their musicianship, shaped by Buck Owens in the studio on a
string of #1 hits, defined the Bakersfield Sound.

What did Buck Owens have in common with Roy Acuff and Ernest Tubb?

He knew what to do with his money. As the funds started to roll in from his hit records, Buck used them to build a music empire for himself. He started Blue Book, a music publisher that controlled his work and that of other country artists, bought radio stations, and set up his own talent management agency.

Fortunately, Buck's business interests were there to support him by the time he stopped having hits in the early 70s. He did get involved in one prominent bit of show business, however. What was it?

Along with Roy Clark, he hosted the *Hee Haw* variety television show on CBS. *Hee Haw* was a cornpone version of the popular *Laugh-In* show, with blackout sketches, running jokes, and a recurring cast of regulars, including Grandpa Jones, Archie Campbell, Minnie Pearl, Stringbean, Junior Samples, and many more. Along with the yucks, viewers were treated to a mix of live and lip-synched performances by many of the hottest country acts of the day. The show was a surprise hit, and stayed on the air either broadcast or in syndication from 1969 to 1994, making it the longest running syndicated television program in history.

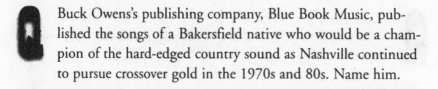

Buck Owens's publishing company, Blue Book Music, published the songs of a Bakersfield native who would be a champion of the hard-edged country sound as Nashville continued to pursue crossover gold in the 1970s and 80s. Name him.

Merle Haggard, born to Oklahoma migrants in Bakersfield in 1937. Like Buck Owens, Merle Haggard also looked to music to save himself from a life of agricultural poverty, and by his late teens was playing in clubs and on the radio.

In his classic hit, "Mama Tried," Merle sings, "I turned 21 in prison, doin' life without parole." True or false?

Mostly true, if a bit exaggerated. Merle's mother was a stern Christian woman who tried to instill her values in her boy; he rebelled instead, and did indeed turn 21 in San Quentin. But he wasn't there for killing anyone. Merle had been caught in a drunken burglary attempt in 1957, and then tried to break out of the county jail, which is why he was sent to prison. He continued to get in trouble while in the pen, but by the time he was released in 1960, he was ready to go straight.

After his release, Merle did odd jobs, but he dreamed of being a musician, and wound up playing bass for Wynn Stewart's band in Las Vegas. He also landed a recording contract with a tiny Bakersfield label. What was his first top-ten hit?

His third single, "(My Friends Are Gonna Be) Strangers," just scratched the bottom of the top ten in 1964. Two years later, he broke into the list three times, with his classic hits "Swinging Doors," "The Bottle Let Me Down," and his first #1 single, "I'm a Lonesome Fugitive."

Beginning with "Okie from Muskogee" in 1969, Merle Haggard developed an image as a superpatriotic reactionary against those who were protesting war and injustice. Did he write "Okie from Muskogee" as a patriotic anthem?

It depends on when you ask him. He has often told reporters that the song was originally intended as a humorous lampoon of small-town yokels. Responding to the song's first line, *We don't smoke marijuana in Muskogee,* Haggard told one reporter, "Son, the only place I don't smoke is in Muskogee." At other times, however, he seemed more than sympathetic to the song's love-it-or-leave-it patriotism, and released other songs in the same vein, most notably "The Fightin' Side of Me."

How many times has Merle Haggard had a song at the top of the country charts?

All of 38, the last being "Twinkle Twinkle Lucky Star" in 1987. He had a particularly good year in 1984, when he had three #1 hits and won a Grammy for his recording of "That's the Way Love Goes."

Their 1968 *Sweetheart of the Rodeo* album marked the first time a popular rock band devoted themselves to a classic country sound. That same year, they even played the *Grand Ole Opry.* Who were they?

Best remembered for their hit folk-rocker "Turn! Turn! Turn!" and the psychedelic anthem "Eight Miles High," The Byrds confused both rock and country audiences with their pioneering album. But band member Graham Parsons was convinced that a blending of country and soft rock sounds would be a musical breakthrough. Imagine the reaction in the Ryman Auditorium when The Byrds walked on stage with long hair and Nudie suits! The album bombed and The Byrds were never invited back to the *Opry,* but they started a trend that would soon sweep through popular music and forever blur the lines between country and rock.

Graham Parsons soon left The Byrds to found the first country rock band. What was their name?

The Flying Burrito Brothers, whose 1969 album, *The Gilded Palace of Sin*, sold poorly but was incredibly influential among the musicians who would soon adopt the classic country sound, including Bob Dylan and the Rolling Stones. Parsons also recorded a solo album released in 1974, *Grevous Angel*, that featured new traditionalist Emmylou Harris.   Parsons died of a drug overdose in 1973, but his impact on rock music was lingering.

Another star had already shocked his fans once by turning from folk music to rock; in 1968, he stunned them again by releasing an album of country songs that even featured a duet with Johnny Cash. Name him.

Robert Zimmerman, better known as Bob Dylan. Dylan had always been a fan of country music (Hank Williams and Slim Whitman were favorites), and had been recording in Nashville studios since 1966. Not only did his 1968 album, *Nashville Skyline*, feature pedal-steel-flavored songs like "Country Pie" and "I Threw it All Away," but Dylan sang them in a syrupy baritone that sounded like a bad imitation of Lefty Frizzell. Dylan didn't get any airplay on country radio, but one of the songs from the album, "Lay Lady Lay," managed to hit #7 on the pop charts.

These Canadians started as a backup band; when they went out on their own, they took their name from the phrase everyone used to refer to them when they performed with Bob Dylan. Their classic sound put rock instruments behind songs that would have been at home on a Carter Family record. Who were they?

 The Band, who recorded and performed from 1967 to 1976. Their biggest hit was the Civil War ballad, "The Night They Drove Old Dixie Down."

 The New Riders of the Purple Sage was another country rock act to get its start in 1969. Three of its members were also members of a popular rock band. What band were they from? And who played pedal steel guitar for the New Riders of the Purple Sage?

 The original Riders featured three members of that acid jam rock icon, the Grateful Dead. That included Jerry Garcia, who was as much a virtuoso on the pedal steel as he was on the electric guitar. While the New Riders were a side project for the Dead band mates, Jerry Garcia's increasing interest in country sounds led the Grateful Dead away from acid rock and toward a more rootsy sound that would intensify the impact country was having on rock.

Roy Acuff, Maybelle Carter, Doc Watson, and Earl Scruggs performed on a 1972 album with a folk rock band who would go on to have several hits on the country charts themselves. What was the band, and from what Carter Family song did the album take its name?

The Nitty Gritty Dirt Band, whose 1970 hit was "Mr. Bojangles," named the album *Will the Circle be Unbroken.* The Grittys didn't just have the classic country legends singing harmony or playing backup; they were front and center on most of the cuts on the three-record set, giving the studio album a real back-porch feel. The success of *Will the Circle be Unbroken* was evidence that there was an enduring audience for old-time country music, one that wasn't being served by the Nashville music machine.

In the early to mid-70s, if you heard a pedal steel guitar on the radio, you might very well have been listening to the Top 40 station. Name the band who had hits with country rock songs like "Desperado," "Take it Easy," and "Peaceful Easy Feelin'."

The Eagles were easily one of the most successful acts of the 70s, with a string of #1 hits and platinum albums. At the same time that Nashville stars were recording disco numbers, the Eagles were proving that twang could still sell.

They had both been part of the Nashville music scene, attempting to accommodate themselves to the pop-oriented sound that dominated country music in the late 1960s. But as rockers began reviving the popularity of classic twang, they grew their hair and created their own synthesis of country and rock. Name these two giants, and identify the movement they founded.

Yes, it was Willie and Waylon, the original Outlaws. We've encountered Mr. Nelson before, crafting classic Nashville songs like "Hello Walls" and "Crazy." But while Willie's songs were big hits for others, a decade spent in Nashville had led to little success in his own recording career. Waylon Jennings had a bit more star power; he started out as a member of Buddy Holly's Crickets, and even managed to have a #2 country hit in 1968, "The Only Daddy That'll Walk the Line." Seeing the success of country rock, both Nelson and Jennings decided to strike out in a new direction, and by 1973 they were allies, demanding artistic control of their recordings and a return to "real" county music.

Where did the term Outlaws come from?

From the song "Ladies Love Outlaws," recorded by Waylon Jennings and included on an album of the same name in 1972. Willie and Waylon teamed up to present an Outlaws show at the 1973 Disc Jockey Convention in Nashville, and in 1974 RCA released a compilation of songs by Willie, Waylon, Waylon's wife Jesse Coulter, and another Music City rebel, Tompall Glaser, entitled *Wanted: The Outlaws.*

Another movement to return to the roots of country paralleled the Outlaws. What's the name given to musicians like Ricky Skaggs, Marty Stuart, Emmylou Harris, Dwight Yoakam, and Iris Dement?

Although each of these greats would probably reject any generic title, they are known as the New Traditionalists. Whether it's traditional acoustic or honky-tonk instrumentation, twangy classic vocal styles, or a devotion to older country songs, each of these artists demonstrates a commitment to exploring country's roots and recapturing a more authentic sound than the more pop-oriented music of stars like Alabama, Garth Brooks, or Shania Twain.

A cover of a Carter Family song provided the name for an album, a Web forum, a magazine, and ultimately a musical movement. What was the song, and who recorded it in 1990?

We're referring to the band Uncle Tupelo's recording of the Carters' "No Depression," which wedded punk sensibilities to country roots. Based on the partnership of guitarist Jay Farrar and bassist Jeff Tweedy, Uncle Tupelo released four albums between 1990 and their breakup in 1994 that specialized in emotionally raw renditions of old country material and original songs that sounded like they could have been recorded in the 1920s. Uncle Tupelo launched a movement originally known as No Depression, and which we now call alt country. Farrar went on to explore country roots with a band named Son Volt.

And what about Jeff Tweedy?

He took most of the members of Uncle Tupelo with him to form the very hot alternative band Wilco.

Who won the Grammy for Best Male Country Performance in 1997?

It was the 65-year-old Johnny Cash, who won the little Victrola for his recording of "The Cage." He followed up the next year with a Best Country Album award for *Unchained*. Johnny Cash had faded to the background in the late 70s and early 80s; but as the demand for more authentic country grew, he experienced a resurgence, first in 1985 as a member of the Highwaymen, and in the late 90s with raw, unpolished recordings of incendiary songs. He suffered from undiagnosed diabetes, which eventually caught up with him; he died in 2003, a few months after his wife, June Carter.

By the way, who were the Highwaymen?

The country supergroup that went on limited tours and released three albums into the early 90s consisted of Cash, Waylon Jennings, Willie Nelson, and Kris Kristofferson. The title cut from the first Highwaymen album went to #1 on the country charts in 1985.

Finish the verse:
For the steel guitars no longer cry
And the fiddles barely play
But drums and rock 'n' roll guitars
Are mixed up in your face
Ol' Hank wouldn't have a chance
On today's radio. . .

. . . Since they committed murder/Down on Music Row.
Alan Jackson and Randy Travis premiered their duet indictment of the Nashville establishment, "Murder on Music Row," at the Country Music Association awards in 1999 before an audience of industry insiders.

What do Jason and the Scorchers, Steve Earle, Whiskytown, and the Old 97s have in common?

They're all among the acts one thinks of as alt country. While the alt country scene encompasses many styles of music, from rockabilly and western swing to gothic punk, its common thread is a reverence for the hard-edged roots of country music. It may not sound much like Hank or Lefty, but Alt Country is evidence that the search for "authentic" country music will continue to invigorate our musical culture for the indefinite future.

In 2001, Merle Haggard recorded an album that mostly contained cover versions. Whose songs did he record?

Roots, Vol. 1 devotes itself mostly to the songs of Lefty Frizzell, with some Hank Williams and Hank Thompson covers, and a few original songs as well. At age 70, Haggard continues to explore his honky-tonk and western swing roots; the new generation of classic country enthusiasts look to him as one of the elder statesmen of hard-edged twang.

Who are "The Last of the Breed"?

Willie Nelson, Ray Price, and Merle Haggard, who released their collaboration album of country standards, *The Last of the Breed*, in 2007.

What do the following acts have in common? Red Allen, Bill Anderson, Asleep at the Wheel, DeFord Bailey, Bobby Bare, Johnny Bond, Bill Boyd's Cowboy Ramblers, The Browns, the Chuck Wagon Gang, Roy Clark, Wilma Lee & Stoney Cooper, Al Dexter, Jimmy Driftwood, The Duke of Paducah, the Everly Brothers, Texas Ruby, the Girls of the Golden West, Woody Guthrie, Stuart Hamblen, George Hamilton IV, Homer & Jethro, David Huston, Ferlin Husky, Stonewall Jackson, Sonny James, Buell Kazee, Jerry Lee Lewis, Hank Locklin, Lonzo & Oscar, the Maddox Brothers & Rose, Jimmy Martin, Clayton McMichen, George Morgan, Moon Mullican, Molly O'Day, Johnny Paycheck, Carl Perkins, Charlie Poole, Charlie Pride, Carson Robinson, Jean Sheppard, Carl Smith, Connie Smith, Red Sovine, The Stoneman Family, Hank Thompson, Justin Tubb, Conway Twitty, Townes Van Zandt, Billy Walker, Speedy West, and Tex Williams.

They are all great classic country stars that I didn't manage to get into this book, and it's only a small sampling of what didn't fit. I'm sorry if I missed your favorites; but thanks to scholars like Bill Malone and institutions like the Country Music Hall of Fame, and to record companies like Rhino that specialize in keeping old music alive, you can launch your own exploration into the country roots tradition, and help make sure that the circle will always be unbroken.